CA

A Novel

Brien Crothers
BMC Publishing
Northern California

All rights reserved. No part of this publication may be reproduced, distributed, or transmitted in any form or by any means, including photocopying, recording, or other electronic or mechanical methods, without the prior written permission of the publisher, except in the case of brief quotations embodied in critical reviews and certain other noncommercial uses permitted by copyright law. For permission requests, write to the publisher at the address below.

18530 Glenwood Road
Hidden Valley Lake, CA 96567
brien@briencrothers.com
Text copyright © 2022 Brien Crothers
Cover designed by MiblArt
Published October 2022
ISBN: 978-1-958637-03-6 (paperback)
ISBN: 978-1-958637-04-3 (e-book)

For the wanderlust in all of us

Praise for Camino Child

"From the moment Summer Darling touches down on the Camino de Santiago pilgrimage route in Spain, you'll fall in love with this strong-willed spirited teen. Camino Child is an amazing story of courage, strength, and perseverance against all odds. Summer is such a strong young woman and it's a pure delight to watch her grow into her power in this beautiful story set on the Camino de Santiago. This one has all the feels! The world needs more Summer Darlings! You won't want to miss Summer's adventurous pilgrimage across Spain. Brien Crothers has created something special with this story."

~ Kevin Craig,
author of The Camino Club

"I enjoyed reading about places on the Camino Francés as it brought back so many lovely memories. I liked the character of Summer Darling, and the author portrayed her as a strong, capable, and intelligent young woman."

~ Meg Maloney,
author of Slow Your Roll: Ruminations & Reflections
On My Walk Across Spain

"The Camino De Santiago is a pilgrimage route which leads to the Cathedral of Santiago de Compostela in Northwest Spain, where it is said the body of the Apostle Saint James is buried. In the Middle Ages Santiago de Compostela was a major pilgrimage destination and millions travelled to pray at the tomb of the Apostle. Whilst because of factors such as the Reformation, plague and war pilgrim numbers eventually dwindled the flow never stopped completely and in the 20th Century there was a great revival of interest which has continued to date. In 2022 it is expected up to 500,000 pilgrims will walk to Santiago."

Johnniewalker Santiago

Georgia's Journal — KEEP OUT
Europe, 1982. This diary is for my third trip to Europe. Freshly graduated from high school, my sister Patricia joins me this time. This her first worldly adventure. (Our sullen little sister, Tilly, will never leave home.)
Our plans: France, Spain, England, wherever the mood takes us.

Inside front cover of Georgia's Travel Journal

<u>ONE</u>

San Sebastián Airport, September 30, 2019

They call me Summer Darling. I call myself an orphan. It seems harsh, I know, since I talk with my parents every few months. Adam and Laura were migrant laborers in the Pacific Northwest, and then I came along. Later, Adam moved us to a commune on the Olympic Peninsula where he could grow marijuana with his friend Paul, the sex-crazed leader of the place they called *The Camp*. Those were terrible years, me constantly arguing with Laura and later dodging Paul's cravings. Then Grandma Pat came and rushed me off to live with her in a small town in Southern California.

Now, Grandma Pat and I are in Spain. Our airplane stutters to a stop at the San Sebastián Airport near the border with France, beside the Atlantic Ocean. The plane and the airport are so small we have to climb down a portable staircase and walk to the terminal. A recent rain has left everything dripping wet, the world smelling as if reborn. You can read all you want about a place, yet not know it. Spain now feels real to me, a true patch of earth with borders and people and a history. All around us, the mountains and their forests, everything lush shades of green, a glaring contrast to home and the dry golden brown of California at this time of year.

We enter the terminal through glass double doors and find the baggage claim area, where we will wait for our backpacks. Two dozen other people, mostly Spaniards, I'd guess, stand too close. Wanting this over as soon as possible I circle the crowd and work my way to the front. After a short wait, a bell rings and the belt squeaks to life. The first through the rubber curtain, an ancient, brown suitcase with worn wheels.

A little old woman with large round glasses slips in beside me. She looks up to meet my eyes and pushes her glasses up the bridge of her nose. I turn away. "Por favor, could you lift the brown one down for me?" I turn back. She looks Spanish—again, I guess—but speaks with an odd, accented English. Okay, so it seems odd to me. What do I know?

"Sure." When it comes to us, I tug at the handle and then spot the red and white HEAVY sticker on one side of the suitcase. I wrench at the weight, mostly dragging it. When it smacks the floor with a thud, I stand the case, wheels down in front of the little lady. She again lifts her round face to me, smiles politely and nods in appreciation, the tight gray curls on her head fixed firmly in place.

Next on the belt, a heap of suitcases surrounding our backpacks. I weed through the suitcases, grab up my pack, and turn to my grandmother. She too has her pack. And a frown souring her face.

"What is it, Grandma Pat?"

"Let's go, Summer."

The little Spanish lady says, "You are *peregrinas*, sí?"

I look back to her, not sure what she means, and wanting to follow my grandmother.

"Pilgrims of the Way. Yes?"

"Oh, sure. We will walk to Santiago," I say. "Walking the Camino del Norte."

"The Way is nearby. My family and I walked this Camino, before I moved to Australia for my work."

"Yes. We have our maps," I say.

"I can show you where the trail begins," she says. "It is close by."

"We'll be fine," says Grandma Pat in her gruff, gravelly voice.

"I must go to the bus stop outside. I can point out the Way to you from there," the woman says to me, then looks down to her suitcase.

I get the message. Grandma Pat has walked away, heading for the automatic doors at the exit, focused on our mission. I pull out the handle and pull the woman's beast of a suitcase toward the door, one of the wheels protests, the other flops out a rhythmic thump, thump.

"Your north coast journey begins on the best kind of day," says the woman who walks beside me. "The warm summer months have passed. In the weeks to come, rain, and later, snow. Fog will hug the shore and lift later each day."

We return to the bright sunlit outdoors. I pull Spanish air deep into my lungs. It is moist and thick, smelling of rose buds and cyclamen flowers. Grandma Pat is halfway across the parking lot. The bus stop is beyond, near the road where it passes the airport.

"We have to finish in Santiago in mid-November," I tell the woman. "Lots of time, my grandmother says."

"What brought you to trek the Camino?"

"Hmm." How much can I tell someone I don't even know?

She glances my way. I feel my heartrate rise and skin flush. "A few weeks ago, some pages torn from a travel journal arrived from an address here in Spain."

What I don't say is that when Grandma Pat opened that envelope and saw the familiar handwriting, her tears surprised us both. The pages from the travel diary were written by her now dead sister, Georgia, my great-aunt. Grandma Pat only let me read the first entry.

"My grandmother," I say as I point in her direction, "had traveled with her older sister, Georgia, to Europe during the summer of 1982. After their time together, her sister returned to Spain to walk the Camino; my grandmother returned to California to start college."

I can't just blurt out everything. My grandmother's beloved sister died of cancer at a young age, while traveling in Asia. I can see Grandma Pat's love for Georgia whenever she speaks of her or reads those few journal pages.

"Checking the package, Grandma Pat found a simple, handwritten note. It read, 'Hay más que aprender.'"

"There is more to learn," says the old woman as she nods her head and looks toward me again. This time with a sad, understanding face.

This conversation takes me back to that day. I could imagine a cascade of questions in my grandmother's mind. I also sensed the pull, a need for her to learn more about Georgia's time in Spain.

"Grandma Pat said we should follow Georgia, find answers if we can. It took no time to convince me. This is why we have come to trek across Spain."

There is another nod of the little woman's head.

She and I reach the bus stop. Grandma Pat waits there, her frown deeper. She is not the most patient person on a normal basis, but I can tell she's more edgy than usual.

"The trail begins down there," says the woman as she points down the busy road. "Near the bridge you can see. Simply follow the *flechas amarillas*, the yellow arrows."

A big man in a uniform takes the woman's suitcase, and we say our goodbyes.

Grandma Pat and I walk side by side, close because of the narrow road. "It *is* a nice day, don't you think?"

"Yes, I do, Summer." She sighs, trying to let go of whatever has her. "Sorry about earlier."

"It has been a long couple of days getting here," I say. She grunts in agreement. "Are you happy to be back?"

With one finger, she slides her glasses down and glares at me along the delicate ridge of her nose. "Yes, of course, silly. I've imagined variations of this moment for almost forty years."

"And here we are," I say with an upbeat tone. She grumbles something I don't catch. "What was that about, earlier, I mean?" These are deep waters I'm treading into.

"Since those pages from my sister's journal arrived, I've been on edge. Who sent them? What's their game?"

"Grandma Pat, why won't you let me read Aunt Georgia's stories?"

"Some private things in there, that's all," she says, then picks up her pace. With nothing more, she has dropped the subject.

Private things? It had seemed like ancient history to me. I fall farther behind while I try to imagine what she may mean, even more curious than before.

We find the trail and see the first splashes of yellow paint. These arrows will lead us to our finish line eight hundred kilometers, five hundred miles, to the west. I don't want to think so far ahead right now, only about finding the next yellow arrow.

At the edge of the road, Grandma Pat stops. She looks down at a splash of yellow paint on the curb, then up to an arrow on a light post. I'm looking at a Camino del Norte app on my smartphone for confirmation. "This is it."

"I know, Summer." She has the handles of her brand-new trekking poles tucked up under her rib cage, sort of leaning on them, and a faraway look on her face. Her eyes glisten, moist.

She stands there so long I begin looking around, batting away my own tears, and taking in our surroundings. Behind us is the airport. Toward the mountains, in this low valley where we walk, are signs of industry and apartment buildings, and before us a hillside covered in vegetation, the roofs of homes and little patches of green fields dotting the broad expanse. High above, trees, thick and luscious when compared to home, coat the crest of the slope. It's only mid-morning, but the air feels warm and thick.

"My sister walked this very path. She often told me to come here, to return to Spain and hike the Camino, visit the cathedrals."

"Why was the journal sent to you now, do you suppose? And why only part of it?" I ask.

"And why such an obscure note? Who sent it? There are so many questions," she says as she stands straight. "We will follow Georgia's spirit and find these answers."

She shrugs her shoulders, lifting and resettling her pack on her hips, and starts walking again. Grandma Pat leads us to a narrow lane beside a stream, then a muddy trail, before returning to another thin strip of road that begins to climb. We have said nothing more. What can we say? We both know the task before us. Baking pies or doing schoolwork or raking leaves can wait. We will walk, only walk, for the next few weeks.

I slow my pace. My backpack rubs a little here and there, pressed into my hips, an odd pull at my shoulders. I fuss with a shoulder strap, then the belt around my waist. Hoping it helps, I shift the whole thing left, then right, pick it up, and settle it back onto my hips.

"You won't even know it's there after a while," says Grandma Pat, ahead of me.

She wasn't even looking my way. Speeding up, I step closer to her. "I'm looking forward to that very thing."

"After a few days, you'll get accustomed to the walking. Everything will settle in, break in. Your pack and shoes only have your very few training miles on them. You'll see." She stays on pace, the titanium tips of her trekking poles clicking on the asphalt. She used to backpack in the mountains near where we live, staying fit and stealing away from people when possible. But it has been a while.

She trudges on, huffing and puffing in choppy rhythm.

I easily catch up to her again. "Are you okay?"

"Still walking, aren't I?"

"Have you taken your pills today?"

"Oh, those damn things," she says. "Your ponytail looks cute, sticking out through your cap. Reminds me of Georgia." Her words trail away and her face droops.

Well, there's the end of any medical discussion.

We pass by homes tucked in among the trees, green fields, and milk cows, and under chestnut trees and evergreens with moss still soggy from the early morning rain. I'll happily let my thirsty skin soak in this goodness. Moving upward, once bathed in sunlight, then ducking into shade, our path comes to an intersection. To our right, a church with a tall steeple, the Camino to our left.

Grandma Pat, still leading the way, heads toward the church. We stroll into the plaza beside the building. From there is a view to the north bathed in brilliant sunlight under a blue sky, puffy white clouds along a soft line of the horizon. We enter the church through a large side door made of dark wood. Inside, the coolness feels wonderful. Grandma Pat takes in the ornate interior of the old place, like she's recording a video in her mind, then takes a photo or two with the camera she inherited from her sister. It's a small digital point-and-shoot camera, its anodized finish worn in spots. She looks around once more, then we leave, returning to the plaza and the warmth of the sun.

"That's France over there, across the river. All those hills you see are Basque Country," Grandma Pat tells me, like she's become my tour guide. She draws in a deep breath, then says, "We'd better get moving."

Our path levels out. My grandmother, the tour guide, continues to report information about what we see. To our left and through gaps in the trees we see more of the Basque hill country and peaks of the Pyrenees mountain range poking up majestically in the background.

We stop for a quick bite of nuts and bars from home, our last few, and absorb the scenery.

"I'd better call Tilly tonight," says Grandma Pat. "Let her know we made it to Europe and found our trail to Santiago."

My great-aunt Tilly, Grandma Pat's younger sister—who isn't all that great, by the way—is the only person she plans to call back home. Tilly lives across "C" Street from us, in Julian, an hour's drive east of San Diego. Before Grandma Pat brought me to live with her, Tilly and her daughter, Lou, short for Louise, moved there. Tilly's husband had left her. Why he ever married her, I'll never understand. She and Grandma Pat could not be more different from one another. Grandma Pat never stops. Tilly never does much of anything, seldom goes anywhere. Her house, built about the same time as Grandma Pat's, falls apart more each day. The yard looks like hell.

Tilly had Lou late in life (only her mother calls her Louise). Grandma Pat told me in secret that Tilly said she got pregnant trying to save her marriage. Which didn't work, but at least there is Lou in our world. We—Lou and I—are close and only a year apart in age. Most people think we are sisters when they first meet us, both tall and blond and pretty, they say. Lou comes over and we help each other with our schoolwork. Lou goes to the local high school. I was used to homeschooling, and Grandma Pat is fine with that. Lou and I often sit on the porch and talk into the evenings. I never go to their place. Tilly likes me about as much as I do her.

My eyes squint and I try to let Grandma Pat's talk of Tilly go, to ignore the fact of an Aunt Tilly in my life.

"Knock it off. She's the only sister I have left," says Grandma Pat. My eyes have given me up.

"I know. I'm sorry." I didn't even know my eyes had a mind of their own.

I make a half-turn to her. "Why . . .? Um, why is she so angry at everything?"

"You reap what you sow."

I have no idea what she means.

"Soon after starting school, Tilly felt inadequate. She was never tall enough, pretty enough, smart enough. It was more, though, I guess. She would never talk about our father. Not that any of us ever did. She has always been angry about her life. But I didn't tell you any of this. Understand?"

I nod, hoping I do.

"We'll stop for the night in the next town. There's a hostel in Pasajes de San Juan, behind the hermitage of Santa Ana," she says, still wearing her tour guide's hat. She's tired from our flight and these first miles of trekking, but her mind remains as sharp as ever. She probably read about it on the plane hours ago. But here, now, she recites it as if straight from her guidebook.

I look at the Norte app. "The *albergue* you mentioned is four miles from here. And it looks like we go downhill most of the way." She frowns and tilts her head slightly downward and to one side glancing over her glasses, a familiar sight. She gets up, shoulders her pack, then squares herself to the trail and moves on. Our plan for today is to only a short hike after so much air travel. After a short distance, and through gaps in the forest, we can see the city of San Sebastián, still miles away. We'll arrive in the large city tomorrow morning. Grandma Pat wants to visit the cathedral there.

Like stepping through a door, we leave the forest path, and weave our way along busy streets and past many homes and apartment buildings. Children play in the street and in neighborhood playgrounds. People walk by us like we aren't even there. I don't mind because I speak little Spanish and zero *Vasco*, the Basque language. But it's like we are ghosts observing life here, no one aware or caring about our presence. Perhaps pilgrims are merely part of the scene, no different from a dog on the prowl or as familiar as a garbage hauler at their work.

Grandma Pat stops in front of a tiny shop. "We should get some supplies. It's probably less than a mile to the hostel." She hasn't yet used the Spanish word for hostel, *albergue*.

Knowing I shouldn't, I want to tease her. Looking down at my phone, I say, "The *albergue* is one-point-one kilometers from here. Less than a mile. And a straight shot through town."

"Let's go see what they have in this place," she grumps. Then she follows that with, "I'm going to throw your damn phone in the river. Which will wipe that grin from your face."

My grin spreads.

With our packs still on, we enter the shop, and carefully ease our way through the narrow aisles. I can still feel it rubbing, pressing in odd, unhappy places. I hope Grandma Pat is right about getting used to the awful thing, and as soon as possible. We pick out things for lunches and snacks. The brands are different, but much of our selection looks yummy.

There's a line of customers at the counter. Grandma Pat

hands me some cash and a string pack, tells me to pay, and steps outside. When it's my turn, I load our things into the simple pack as the checker slides them to me. When she has finished, I collect the change, thank the woman, and join my grandmother outside. She has taken off her backpack, it's leaning against a signpost.

"Are you—"

"I'm fine. Let's go," she barks and lifts her pack.

San Sebastián, Spain

July 17, 1982

I left Patricia in London, waiting for her flight home. Missing her already. I woke in San Sebastián, an overnight bus from Madrid. Visited the Buen Pastor Cathedral, nestled and pure in the center of this quaint city beside the Bay of Biscay. Bought a postcard of the Buen Pastor to send home. I cannot explain my admiration for such grand old buildings, but I hope Pat visits this one someday.

From Georgia's Travel Journal

TWO

Pasajes de San Juan, September 30, 2019

In fifteen minutes, we are at the front door of our first albergue. It's an old building made of large blocks of stone and has two large symbols on the wall facing us as we stroll up. One is a seashell, a symbol for the Camino. The other is a Basque symbol I know even less about. It looks like a propeller from a boat but I'm sure it holds other meanings.

A tall, bulky man stands at the door with his back to us, blocking the way, a faded backpack at his feet, next in line to check in. Inside, I can see the host sitting behind an old, wooden desk logging a different pilgrim into a thick, worn ledger. He, the host I mean, is a round bald man, looking officious but he jokes with the woman pilgrim before him.

Beside the woman stand two others, her friends I assume, or a sister and their mother. She speaks in hesitant Spanish to the man. Then she turns and speaks in accented English to the man behind her. Her accent seems Russian. She and the others have enormous packs. Grandma Pat had warned me about over packing. Their packs are easily twice as big as ours. Probably twice as heavy too.

The heat from the direct afternoon sun bears down on us as if from an open oven door at Grandma Pat's café back home. She offloads her pack and sits down on the steps leading to the door. Falling away from her grip, the pack rolls to one side. She leaves it, disgust at its defiance and a tiredness in her eyes. I set my pack down against the block wall, loosely tie our string pack of groceries to it, and stand Grandma Pat's pack against mine. From the doorway we hear, "Next."

After a few moments, it's our turn, and we go inside and hand over our pilgrim credentials and passports. The passports I knew about, of course. But the pilgrim credential was a new concept to me. We need them to stay in these pilgrim-only hostels. You also collect stamps in their pages so you can earn a Compostela, a certificate of completion, when finished with your Camino. When the host says *siete euros*, seven euros, I can't believe my quick currency conversion. Grandma Pat pays him and takes back our passports and credentials.

With the formalities out of the way and wanting to avoid more climbing, we take the last two bottom bunks in the dorm on this level and set our packs down. Grandma Pat eases onto her bunk. Her eyes are weary. As soon as she knows I am looking at her, a look of determination returns to her face, and she peers across the dark, narrow space to meet my appraising eyes.

"I am fine. Just need a minute's rest," she says. "I've spent a lifetime on my feet, but today they hurt like hell."

"My feet ache too. Something feels hot under one of my big toes and the metatarsal bones ache in both of my feet."

"I have bought you other books, girl," she says. And she has. Wonderful books. But I like anatomy. The camp where I lived had only one book before they brought me textbooks for home schooling. That one book, a tattered copy of Sobotta's Atlas of Human Anatomy, and I spent a lot of time together.

"I know you did," I say.

"We should look at your hotspot though." She settles back and closes her eyes, meaning we'll do it later. I leave her to rest and go exploring our home for the night.

I shower and rinse out socks and underwear to hang on a line behind the albergue. Those chores done and back inside, I run into Grandma Pat. She has recovered some of her color.

"Summer, go ask our host where we can find a place to get a sit-down meal."

"The hosts are called *hospitaleros* or *hospitaleras*, Grandma Pat."

"Yes, lovely. Now go ask."

Following his directions down a succession of steep, twisting staircases we come to a port-side cobblestone street. Literal cobblestones, which are awkward to walk on, especially with sore feet. We enter the first restaurant we come to. The mouth-watering aroma of garlic simmering in olive oil fills the air. I gulp down a flood of saliva. We choose a table in one corner of the quiet place and wait for the man behind the bar to notice we are here. While he decides on our worthiness, I pull out my smartphone. As we had climbed down those many stairs, I remembered some bit of information in the Camino app.

In a few moments I find what I'm looking for. "This app has all the Camino towns. It shows if there are albergues, places to eat, stores, other things for pilgrims."

"So does my guidebook," Grandma Pat says.

Finally, the man comes to take our order. He's not nearly as friendly as Juan, our *hospitalero*. We point at the meals we have chosen from the menu and Grandma Pat orders some red wine. My eyes lift in an involuntary glance. They shouldn't have. Yep, here it comes.

"You'd better keep your opinions to yourself, girl."

The man returns to his kitchen.

"Sorry." I turn the phone to point out more of what I have found. "This has up-to-date information. Here's a comment from someone who ate here yesterday. They have little good to say about the food."

"Too late now, Summer. I guess I won't throw your phone in the river," she says. "Not quite yet." She smiles her pretty smile I love so much, yet see so little of, and she tucks her hair behind one ear.

Our meal is flavorful and filling; I can't agree with last night's reviewer.

We hike back to the albergue by a different—just as vertical —route. The age of our surroundings, the hodgepodge arrangement of stairways, and the apartments with families on their tiny verandas are so very different from what I see in California. The place has a friendly feeling, though. Almost at home, welcoming.

Grandma Pat walks well behind me, having a hard time with the climb. She has looked so tired since we stopped for the day. She says it's jet lag and trail miles, she's fine.

We find our bunks as darkness settles upon the port town. Chill, moist air flows from the sea through an open window. I get cozy in my sleeping bag, close my eyes, and wait for the lights to go off. Grandma Pat goes to brush her teeth. When she returns, she kneels beside me. I feel the warmth of her, can still smell the wine on her breath, but I keep my eyes closed. She zips my bag up a little more and tucks it in around my neck. I fall asleep with a smile in my heart.

Next morning, I wake to the rustling of plastic bags. Then

something heavy hits the hardwood floor of the room above. I open one eye, looking for the window above me overlooking the bay. Dawn barely breaks the night sky, a slight grayness above an orange glow of port lights below. I catch the scents of sea and diesel fumes and fish wafting through the old stone building.

The other eye reluctantly opens, and I look toward Grandma Pat's bunk. She's not there, her pack gone, the bunk empty. My chest squeezes tight. I hurry out of my sleeping bag. Dropping my feet to the cool floor, they feel the texture of the ancient wood, its many cracks and twists worn smooth by the zillion pairs of feet before mine. I slide off the bunk and pull on a hoodie, one long enough to cover my ass, and in bare feet begin to search for my grandmother.

She sits on the floor in the laundry room outside of the bathrooms, the contents of her pack spread out in a single layer before her. She looks up as I enter the room. She squints her eyes.

"I can't find my damn glasses," she grumbles as she looks back to her possessions.

I know she's not blind without them, but she'll need them to read road signs or her favorite guidebook. I ask questions about where she has looked.

"Don't you think I would have thought of that?" she huffs. I keep quiet. "Get yourself ready to go. They'll turn up. Or they won't."

One of the Russian women climbs down the stairs and asks if my grandmother has found her glasses. How long has Grandma Pat been looking for them? The woman's accent is more distinct than her daughter/friend/whatever. Grandma Pat, never lifting her face, says, "No," and continues with her search. She slowly inspects each item, then sets it on a pile beside her empty backpack.

Another Russian woman arrives, the younger one we saw checking in on our arrival yesterday. She slowly descends the stairs. I see an odd look on her face. I guess you'd call it a sheepish look. Grandma Pat senses this somehow and looks in the woman's direction.

"Are these your glasses?" the woman asks as she extends a hand. The older Russian moves to her side. Does she think my grandmother will attack her daughter/friend/whatever? Not so sure she won't, I feel my shoulders raise up toward my ears and my hands become fists.

Grandma Pat struggles to rise from the floor and stand, groaning from the effort.

She steps up close to the two women. "Oh, yes, That's them. Where did you find them?" she asks in a light tone. I know her tones. It's not as cheerful as the Russians might think.

"They were in my glasses case. I'm sorry," says the younger woman. "I thought they were mine in the darkness last night."

"No harm done. I'm happy we found them," says Grandma Pat as she reclaims them, slips them onto her face, and tucks her short hair behind her ears. There she is. She still looks tired, but a smile creases her pretty face. Old as she may be (I've never raised the question), she is still an attractive woman. At least that's what the men who come into the café for a slice of her famous apple pie say about her.

The tension in the air eases. The Russians quietly leave the room, and I go back to my bunk. It's time to get dressed, store my sleeping bag, and find places for our food supplies in my backpack. It's still dark outside but I can now make out clouds filling the sky. Gray and so flat-bottomed they seem to have settled softly onto a glass ceiling not far above the town.

Others get up from their bunks. They start stretching and yawning, sorting, and packing their gear. The space I need for comfort fills with their activity. I quickly tuck the last bits into my pack and slip past them. Grandma Pat waits.

To get to the other side of Pasaia Bay, a boat makes regular trips across the channel. I stumble aboard and grip a handrail. Have I ever ridden in a boat? Still holding tight, I look to my grandmother. She has a stoic, been-there-done-that look about her. A man motors us to the other shore not far away, collecting a few euro cents for the passage from each of us. The chug-chug of a smelly diesel engine pushes the craft along the calm water. There are people my age going to school, a couple of men wearing neat suits, and two other pilgrims. It is early, we are quiet.

At the dock, the boater ties his craft to a cleat and helps each of us to shore.

"Let's find some breakfast," Grandma Pat commands and heads off.

I follow. In a few blocks, we find a plaza. The first café is full of fishermen and haggard, bent old men, only one woman working behind the counter. My grandmother takes a wide path around a half-dozen men talking loudly on the sidewalk at the restaurant's entrance. From inside emanates the loud harshness of too many deep voices all yammering at once.

"Let's keep looking," says Grandma Pat. "And if we see an ATM, let's get you some cash."

"Right behind you. God, I thought it got loud in your café back home, in Julian."

No response; my grandmother on task. We cross the plaza, walk around a street corner, and see another café. A quiet one. One little woman with short, curly white hair sits at a table, a younger one busily cleans tables.

"This will do," Grandma Pat says.

We select something made of eggs and potatoes from under a glass case and order cups of *té negro*, black tea, for me and *café con leche*, coffee with steamed milk, for Grandma Pat. The portions of *tortilla*, as the woman called it, steam hot when she delivers them to our table. I catch an aroma of grilled onions in the savory mix.

Saliva fills my mouth again. This is not like our tortillas in California. It's more like a crustless quiche made of eggs, potatoes, and onions, cut into segments like a pie.

Grandma Pat lowers her nose so close to the coffee I worry she'll dive in. She draws steam deep into her maxillary sinus and lets out a sigh of utter satisfaction.

So tasty and perfect for this morning, we eat our slices of tortilla in silence. Grandma Pat reviews the information in her guidebook. I'm memorizing the route out of town shown on my phone. The map shows a line—our path—up long stairways and along trails out of town and into a forest, then country lanes most of the way to San Sebastián, a few miles away. As I finish my breakfast, I open my Camino app to the correct place and write a quick review about our fantastic breakfast. Maybe I was just hungry.

Afterward, we find an ATM. Grandma Pat stops in front of the machine. "Hand me my wallet. It's in the pouch on top of my pack."

I pull at a zipper to open the pouch and extract her wallet. I flip its bi-fold sections open in my palms; the contents of the wallet exposed for her. She studies the ATM.

"Which card do you want?" I say as I count the many cards.

Without looking, she says, "The credit union debit card."

I read names as I look down the long selections of cards. I reach for one.

"No, not that one," she says turning back to me. "The green one."

"Why does it matter?"

"You must tell them what country you'll travel to, or the card won't work, for security reasons. Jenn, down at my credit union, showed me and Tilly how to do that online. She's on my account, I'm on hers."

After her transaction, Grandma Pat hands me some euro bills to stick in my pocket for when I need them.

"So, not all of those cards will work here?"

"No," she replies.

"So why did you bring the others?"

"I won't next time. I knew better, but it's habit to have everything with me."

I return the wallet to its pouch, and we start to walk. Gray fog high above keeps the sun off us for now, and the trail steepens as we climb away from Pasaia Bay. My grandmother is slower this morning. Yesterday took a lot more out of her than she admitted, and even more than I had suspected. Our route leads up a narrow chain of stairs cut into a solid rock hillside. A simple pipe railing lines the outer edge. Below, miniature waves lap against the cliff face.

I am right behind her, so close the bill of my cap almost touches her backpack. She pushes off using her trekking poles. Occasionally they slip from the smooth surface of the stairs and come at me. I stop for a moment and watch her slow progress. She is short of breath and exhales in ragged fits.

At the top, the views out to sea and along the coast are spectacular. Fishing boats leave the harbor, pass through a narrow exit, and plow their way into the glass-smooth surface of open waters. Long freighters are pasted onto the horizon line.

Grandma Pat stops and leans on her poles.

"Did you take your pills this morning?"

She ignores me and, after catching her breath, she starts walking again.

I give her a few moments and then catch up to her.

She glances over at me. "Remember what I said about wanting to stop at the cathedral in San Sebastián? Georgia told me many times to visit the cathedrals when I 'Finally get around to going on Camino.' She said it again in her journal, like she knew I would one day read those pages. She always pushed my buttons," says Grandma Pat, as we stop for another break, take in the view, and greet other pilgrims as they pass us by.

Georgia was Grandma Pat's only idol, the only other person in the world she has ever looked up to, it seems. Georgia was an adventurer, in every sense of the word. She and Grandma Pat went to Europe together. When Grandma Pat settled down, Georgia went right on traveling. She served tables in Greece, worked as an assistant mountain guide in Washington state, and drove to Patagonia in an old Land Cruiser with a boyfriend in the 1990s.

"Yes, of course," I finally respond. "Eat lunch on the beach afterward?"

"Lunch on the beach sounds damn good," she replies. "Something special to look forward to."

San Sebastián, Spain
July 18, 1982
Needing a job and a place to stay for a while, I find both. My Spanish is terrible, and many people here speak the Basque language, but being able to talk with British tourists secured the job. I wait tables, clean rooms, and talk with the tourists at a beach spa/hotel.

From Georgia's Travel Journal

THREE

San Sebastián, October 1, 2019

Above San Sebastián we see the city center and two arches of amber-colored beach bound by points of land jutting out into the Bay of Biscay. Our path, lined here and there by dense green foliage, descends along narrow blacktop lanes, winding this way and that. In the distance, I point out the bell tower of the cathedral. I see a hint of a smile form on my grandmother's face. I can only hope she will rest for a while at the beach, take a nap. We don't know what we will find as we follow Georgia's journal west across Spain, but Grandma Pat has told me we have plenty of time to finish this trek to Santiago, time to make our flight home.

Though I smell a hint of rain, the clouds above us open to patches of blue beyond the fluffy white. "It may get warm this afternoon," I say to her back. Focusing on the path, she says nothing in reply, the metal tips of her trekking poles tapping out a slow rhythm on the hard surface. My brand-new ultra-lite poles are still tied to my backpack.

Nearly noon by the time we enter the city, I realize how slow we are walking this morning. Much slower than yesterday. I set the thought aside. We still move forward.

First, though, *Catadral del Buen Pastor,* the Cathedral of the Good Shepherd. This is my grandmother's thing. She's the one who wants to visit the cathedral. But I do feel an excitement knowing we are getting close to the place Georgia wrote about. Following directions on my smartphone, we walk beside a river with a name as long as your arm and impossible for me to pronounce, then turn right and along a busy street. Though I can see the cathedral on the map, we don't see the real thing until the street comes to a plaza. The area opens like flower petals blooming. The tree-lined plaza has patches of lawn. People sit on benches eating a bite, chatting with friends or coworkers.

"This cathedral is of Gothic Revival design," Grandma Pat says. "I never studied them, but Georgia had a thing for churches and knew all the architectural styles used in Europe, if not the world."

As we come closer, we see scaffolding and safety netting covering much of the face of the grand old building. The noise of drills and hammering drifts from every conceivable part of the work. A palpable look of disappointment shades Grandma Pat's face. Beads of perspiration coat her brow.

Almost reluctantly, she first leads the way around the outside of the cathedral, scanning skyward, then back to ground level. Up and down her face goes in slow motion as we stroll beside the golden sandstone walls and buttresses, and below small gothic spires, each topped with a lichen-coated stone cross. I have never seen anything like this. Nothing this old, ornate, or proud. I feel Georgia's love for such grandeur enveloping me. I never knew her, but I appreciate her love of such buildings, the things human beings can create.

Finished with our survey of the outside, we've circled back to the front entrance. I look at my grandmother. She continues her appraisal of the stonework, grimaces when another machine comes to life, then peers through the wide legs of scaffolding and into the immense structure. We move through the entrance. The noise of loud machines emanates from behind tacky, tattered blue tarps. Her displeasure with the intrusion grows into frustration. She would burst if someone crossed her right now. I back off a half step, or more.

Inside, the mechanical racket is still present, but muted. Grandma Pat shuffles left, stopping for a moment. She slowly, purposefully folds her poles and secures them to her backpack as she scrutinizes this new environment. Sweat lays traces on her cheeks. She begins to walk past the various features set along the long wall. Watching her go, I hope she will remember to take a break. I drift away on my own tour and step up to a column rising from the floor and reaching up to a magnificent, arched span of the ceiling high above. The column is carved from stone and humongous. It's the size of trees—the largest ones—in the forest where I played as a kid. I now see why we made the detour from the Camino path to come here.

I continue making my way forward and toward where the priests deliver their sermons. Stained-glass windows occupy much of the space high above me. A soft light comes through. The clouds have closed in again.

There are worshippers—all of them women—sitting, looking down. They are in prayer. I guess they are, each of them reading prayers or something from smartphones propped up in their hands. *See, Grandma Pat, even the church has gone high tech.*

I let go of the thought and work my way into an area reaching out to the side of the cathedral. High above, an enormous circular stained-glass window fills a wide space under a pointed arch. The opposite extension of the enormous building holds a mirrored view. To my left, an ornate, velvety red carpet climbs a few steps to the altar.

It's like I'm in a movie camera, taking in images I have never considered before. I hear a thud, sense it vibrate through me. I ignore the interruption. There's a shuffle, a slide of shoe on stone behind me. Then a loud gasp cracks my trance. Shocked back to an awareness of my surroundings, I turn and see a woman standing over my grandmother. Grandma Pat sags over her backpack in a pew not twenty feet from where I stand. Her water bottle lies at her feet. So deep in my spell as I took in my new surroundings, I had no idea my grandmother sat close by.

It slowly penetrates my skull the woman standing over her was the one who had passed behind me and startled me when she gulped for air. She backs away and crosses herself. What is her problem? Another lady, a large arrangement of flowers in her hands, quickly heads for a door leading into a dark room. I can hear her call out, not what she has said. My feet weigh a ton, my legs stiff as posts, and my backpack digs deeper into my shoulders. With an unexplainable effort, I walk toward Grandma Pat. I slowly slip past the gasper to sit beside my grandmother.

As I shrug off my pack, I hear muffled words from the dark room. The voices seem inhuman, ghostly; words in Spanish I cannot recognize, coming from a distance too far away, muted by thick stone walls, and in a tone I don't want to understand. I let my pack go, and it rolls off the pew, bounces quietly off a padded kneeling board and onto the floor. I wrap an arm around Grandma Pat, and it hits me. Everything I had been ignoring for the last few moments, all the hints at what I had missed, come crashing down on me. I draw her in, returning her to the seatback. Her pack, too, rolls over, bounces, and falls to the stone floor with a loud thump, a bookend to mine. She is as white and bland as an unbaked pie crust, perspiration glistening on her cheeks and forehead. With my other hand, I set each of her hands in her lap. They are clammy, cool, creepy. How can they be so cold—so fast? A shiver runs up from my seat and I begin to shake uncontrollably.

I'm just a kid, I think to myself, the thought quick as a rifle shot. How can I be so sure she is dead? How can I know what her clammy, white skin might mean? Thankfully, her eyes are closed. She looks so peaceful, despite the ghastly pallor. I have never seen her so happy, so ... relaxed?

"Well, crap, of course she's relaxed."

I realize I have said these words out loud—in a church. *No, stupid, it's a cathedral.*

The incomprehensible voices are now at my side, in front of me, and on the other side of my grandmother. Our packs get moved aside. Whoa. Wait. What? Everything we have is in those backpacks. Passports, credit cards, everything. I react, then recoil. *That doesn't matter right now,* the voice inside my head mumbles, as if I should know better.

A woman—the one with the flowers before—sits beside me and wraps an arm around me, like I am with my grandmother. The aroma of fresh-cut flowers teases my senses. A tall man in a long brown robe, a black leather belt around his middle, stands on the other side of my grandmother. He touches her neck, then his thin, white fingers encircle her wrist. He slowly stands back and makes the form of a cross on his chest, then wraps a broad ribbon around his neck and takes out a small leather-bound book.

I'm about to scream when he finally finishes whatever he is doing. I push the woman away, harder than I should have, and look up into the man's face. He asks me a question in English. Even in my language, I don't want to hear his words. He takes a moment and walks around the pews to replace the flower lady. As they pass, I hear him speak with her in a calm voice. The only words I catch are *policia, teléfono,* and *medico.*

He sits down and takes my hands in his. They are warm, and he smells musty, sort of like wet wool. "Your mother?" I hear the calm tone in his question. A second time he has asked, I realize.

"My grandmother," I answer, and look back to her peaceful face.

"I am sorry, my child. Your grandmother has gone to heaven now."

His English is good. So good, I'm not sure of his origins.

"I am Father Ernesto. Where are your parents? Are they or others with you?"

His words ooze in slow procession past my concerns over his nationality and his occupation. He is a priest. *Well, of course he's a priest, girl. Look at his robes.* His English is so good. Is he from here? *Who cares where he is from?* He has the telltale monk's circle of hair around a bald spot atop his head. Who cuts in that style for monks, anyhow? *What do you go on about, child?*

"My parents are dead," I say with the confidence of having said this a hundred times before. "It's only the two of us. We walked here on the Camino del Norte."

"Señora Rosa, the parish secretary, has gone to call the authorities. They will arrive and help us through this. Do you want to pray with me?"

"No, Father. I am not catholic, not religious."

"Of course, my child. I will stay with you, either way."

My child? I'm not a child. Or I am? I'm just a kid. What do I know about any of this? As quick as a faucet being turned on, silky-smooth tears stream down my face and onto the pile of our hands. He doesn't flinch or move in the slightest. I am unnerved by my tears falling onto him. I turn away and to my grandmother again. She is still there, still calm, and peaceful, now ashen gray. The perspiration on her face has mostly evaporated.

Something high above us catches my attention. The clouds have relented. The round stained-glass window to the right of us glows in a brilliant display of colors. A rainbow effect casts across the space to splash upon the far wall. As I take in the sight, focusing only on the round shape of a rose, this amazing display takes my breath away, the light seeming to bounce toward me as if from a prism, and penetrating everything, making me one with the world.

The man beside me follows my gaze, then says, "The builders, and perhaps God, meant for this scene to inspire us."

Paralyzed by everything that has happened in the last few minutes, I look back to him. "She didn't get to enjoy lunch on the beach."

San Sebastián, Spain
July 25, 1982
Working and living near the beach, even in this quiet corner of the world, certainly has its perks. Young, tan, fit Spanish men far outnumber the fat, old Brits who bellow at me from across the veranda. "Gin and tonic, sweetie, no ice, no slice." Their wives shake their heads at the men, as the old coots watch me walk away

From Georgia's Travel Journal

<u>FOUR</u>

San Sebastián, October 1, 2019

Grandma Pat's body lies on a gurney, a cold white sheet draped over her. A man and a woman dressed in tasteless green and yellow uniforms with reflective stripes cover my grandmother's face and fuss with the sheet here and there. The *policia*, the cops, ask a million questions of me and a few of Father Ernesto. They have my grandmother's passport, but I can't find mine. I am getting as mad as my grandmother would have. Frustrated, I bellow, "Why do you need my passport right this damn minute?"

They flinch at my indiscretion here in Catedral del Buen Pastor.

In a flurry, I go through my grandmother's things, her pack at my feet. The thought of ripping through her possessions grips my guts. Where did that stupid bag go? I had the stupid thing a minute ago. I find another bag. It holds the pages from Georgia's journal. I pull out a light jacket, then my grandmother's raincoat.

My Grandma Pat is dead, gone, but right there, cold. I feel hot, flushed. Tears burn behind my eyes then gush from their home, streaming down my fiery face. An odd question blooms from my infuriation: Will I see steam boiling up before my eyes?

I need one thing: Tilly's phone number. As much as I hate the idea, I need her right now. Finally, I find the bag. It hid from me under the backpack, on the floor. It contains Grandma Pat's notebook, everything to me at this moment. Tilly's contact information glares at me from inside the cover, EMERGENCY NUMBER written above it. I feel sad that Tilly is the only person Grandma Pat would have someone call in a crisis.

Handing the notebook to one of the cops, I show him the phone number and say, "llama la," call her. I imagine Mr. Penito, the Spanish tutor my grandmother had hired for me, standing at my side. *"Ella es su hermana,"* she is her sister, I say, pointing to the gurney. I can't believe the Spanish words came so easily. They are there, rolling off my tongue like a native speaker when I needed them most. They all look at me with a questioning look. *"Hablo un poco Español. Muy poco."* That I speak a little Spanish seems to satisfy them for the moment. That and my aunt's phone number. They seem pleased to have someone older to talk with about this situation, even if this person lives halfway around the world. I'm sure they will want me to call her first, to break the bad news about her sister. Crap.

At least they no longer pester me for my stupid passport every two seconds. Now I remember which pouch I put it in. I pull it out and hand the passport over.

The cops say something, first one then another, nodding at each other like agreeing fools. The words fly at me at rapid-fire speed, like all of a sudden I speak and understand the language fluently. I lower my head in frustration.

Father Ernesto comes close to my side. "They want you to go with them to make the call to your great-aunt and start the process of returning your grandmother to the States. Your aunt will need to come here to San Sebastián and claim h—"

"She's not all that great," I blurt out, immediately sorry I have. I change my tone, "Will you go with me, Father, to the police station, I mean?" I realize I feel like a helpless child again, that I need someone to hold my hand. I have a hard time trusting people, but this man— *He's a priest, silly.* He seems all right.

Where I grew up, most of the adults spent their lives so stoned or drunk they could barely tie a shoelace. Michael was my only friend—if you could call him a friend. He was younger than me, and the only other kid in camp. Though feral as a wildcat when Adam moved Laura and me to the forest, he was smarter than most of the adults. None of them—except Michael—were worthy of my trust, especially their lecherous leader Paul.

"I shall meet you there. The police dislike meddlers, but I have many friends in their ranks," says Father Ernesto with confidence.

Tall as I am, I have to lean back and lift my face to peer into his calming brown eyes and say, "Thank you, Father."

Once the pressure of the previous moments, the questioning by the cops, Grandma Pat being handled like a sack of potatoes, and the stressful search for my passport have slipped away, I sense my surroundings again. The cathedral's vastness has gone. The walls have closed in on me. Visitors and parishioners come and go. Other police officers keep the onlookers away. The gasper, the lady who had discovered my grandmother's body, sits in a pew a few rows back, kneeling and praying. Needing a minute and looking to the cop who seems in charge, I raise a finger, then point my chin toward the woman. He seems to struggle with the delay but understands.

I walk to her, bend to one knee, and put a hand on hers. They are warm and soft. She says something softly in Spanish I can't translate but understand fully. We stand and hug each other.

This special moment helps us both. The flower lady, the secretary, joins us. The grasper and I take her hands in ours. Father Ernesto knows better than to intrude.

I have never felt more mature or clearer on what my grandmother would have me do. Of the future, she would say only one thing, "Get on with it, girl."

San Sebastián, Spain
July 26, 1982
Spent my day off at the beach with Mr. Garcia's son, Pepe. Garcia owns the resort where I am working. Pepe works there too. He's sweet, but a little clingy, needy.

From Georgia's Travel Journal

FIVE

San Sebastián, October 1, 2019

In the backseat of a car, sunlight lays on my lap where I sit with Father Ernesto. The past few hours play over and over in my mind.

The call to Tilly and Lou was the hardest thing I have ever done. In hysterics, she handed the phone to Lou. We talked for a few minutes. Before getting off the line, Lou said she would help her mother with a flight to San Sebastián.

Now, the priest's car passes the river with the too-long name. His driver smells of tobacco smoke and greasy sausages. My hands, the skin white in the sun's rays, lay in my lap detached from my awareness. Pale whites will always remind me of my grandmother's passing. I squish my eyes closed as hard as possible, forcing the image away, and I quietly sob once more. Opening them again, hoping to find something else to focus on, I find the man in the front seat.

A silly fact settles in: Father Ernesto has his own driver. He is driving us back to the cathedral.

"Rudolfo is a volunteer." Father Ernesto heard those thoughts rattling around in my skull. "Once a priest, Rudolfo has recently retired. Helping out the diocese where he can keeps him in touch with old friends and offers him continued purpose."

Rudolfo glances over his shoulder to me with a soft smile filled with stained and gapped teeth, and he nods. I smile back, then turn and look out the window. It surprises me the number of buses on the streets as we leave the river's edge and make left and right turns up one street and down another. There are few cars. Having all these buses has to keep the traffic down. Why do I care about the traffic patterns of San Sebastián? I have a bigger problem: Tilly is coming here, coming to Spain. And I have to wait for her.

"You will need a place to stay, my child," says Father Ernesto in his kind voice. "An acquaintance of mine owns a *pensión*, a guest house, not far from the Buen Pastor. If you like, I can inquire about a room and ask Rudolfo to take you there."

"I guess I don't have much of choice, do I, Father?"

"It is a clean place. They are good people. There are cafés and restaurants nearby. And a safe place to stay," he answers, as he sees then nods his head to an acquaintance outside as the car slowly rounds a street corner.

"How long before I can go, do you think?" My question comes out sounding weaker than I had hoped.

"It will depend on when your great-aunt arrives, and when the authorities have completed their tasks."

I turn to him and him to me. "I'm going to walk the Camino for my grandmother, Father Ernesto."

He turns away and looks again to the city passing by. He considers this news, my words. Grandma Pat always said things like "You can see the wheels turning in there." I never really understood that sentiment or truly appreciated its meaning until right this minute.

Deep in thought, focused, he eventually turns and says, "I cannot say if it is allowed or the right thing for you to do now, my child."

"You say 'my child' a lot, Father. Sometimes, that's exactly how I feel. Like a child, like I am only a kid. Not now, though. I'm gonna finish this trek for my grandmother. When I needed her, she came for me. She packed me and my things into her car and drove me twelve-hundred miles back to California to live with her. She needed my help, too. I worked at her café each day after my studies were done. We needed each other. Now, I will do what she set out to do, learn about her sister's journal and walk to Santiago. She taught me we always finish what we start."

He looks into my eyes, searching. I do not know what he expects to find. Is he considering my reasoning, seeing if I mean it, if I have what it takes? I think they call it "mettle." Do I have the mettle?

"I have to arrive in Santiago by the tenth of next month. And I will walk there for my grandmother," I say with all the conviction I can draw up from inside. My heart hurts, but the voice in my head says, *Do this. What else have you got to do?*

"Take some time, talk with your grandmother's sister. Make your choice, then. That is my only guidance, Summer."

He has called me by my given name. He didn't even know it until the lead cop looked at my passport and said, "Summer Darling." The man's accent made my name sound different. It came out warm and airy, sort of glamorous. And it made me feel older, though the cop quickly pointed out my young age. He did the math and said my age aloud. I was as quick to say my birthday was coming soon, my sixteenth, in a few weeks. Not exactly satisfied, I don't think, the officer handed my passport over to Father Ernesto.

Father Ernesto was surprised by my years, and more surprised to have been given this responsibility for my wellbeing.

Most people think I'm older than I am. My height says one thing to them, and a confidence earned of an odd upbringing adds to my cover. But the actual number of years say something entirely different.

"Thank you, Father. I will think about what you said. Either way, I hope I can come see you before I go," I say as I look at his kind face.

"Of course, my— Yes, Summer. Any time you like." From under his robe, he pulls out an ancient wallet, the leather checked and torn at the corners. He removes a blue rubber band, opens the wallet, and pulls out a business card. The card simple, only his name and a phone number. "If calling me from your phone, include the Spanish country code, three-four."

"Thank you, Father Ernesto," I say again as I take the card. I cannot thank this man enough. I know of his profession, and I can see his compassion for others, his empathy for me. Not everyone, not even all priests, I imagine, show such kindness.

"You will need this too," he says as he hands over my passport. "They will need it at the pensión tonight. Foreign visitors must provide their whereabouts."

I look into his eyes. I see a message there, and trust. I nod my head, understanding his meaning, understanding I should not take off for Santiago without him knowing.

After the cathedral, Rudolfo delivers me to the Pensión Ortiz. Politely ignoring my protests, he carries my backpack and my grandmother's backpack inside the building. He sets the packs down, leaning them against the check-in counter. He makes certain Father Ernesto's friend receives me. Mr. Ortiz greets us both, then turns to me. Quiet as a mouse, Rudolfo slips away.

For the first time since arriving in Europe, I feel unsure of my surroundings. I'm alone. The awareness of this fact stabs at me. A gravity sets on me like never before and a pain runs from my left shoulder blade to my right foot. I know it's not real, but it feels as if someone has shoved a long blade through me.

"Father Ernesto, he tell me what happens," says Mr. Ortiz as he lowers his face and crosses himself.

Paolo Ortiz is a short, round man. His hairy belly hangs out from under a tight-fitting polo shirt. He takes my passport for the register, then eases it back across the desk.

The little blue book, the thing I need most right now, crisp, and new, still lays flat as the day it arrived in the mail earlier this year. Grandma Pat wanted me to have one "Just in case" and helped me with the paperwork. We had talked of driving to Mexico, but never did. She wanted to visit an old friend in Canada, but never made the time. She never will. Not now.

"I show you room now," says Mr. Ortiz, bringing me back to the moment.

The room sparkles clean and smells of lemon oil and flowers. Mr. Ortiz sets down my grandmother's backpack and leaves. I close the door, happy to close off the outside world. I place my pack on a well-worn luggage stand. First things first, I begin stripping. I have worn these clothes for nearly four days. They stink, but more to the point, they hurt, clinging too tightly to me, strangling me. I need space and to peel away all that has happened. And I'll take a hot shower.

After I shower and wash my hair, I lie down on the bed. The covers have a lavender fragrance. A Mrs. Ortiz? A thin smile tries to take over my gloomy frown. The blare of an odd sounding siren turns down our street and passes by. A wave of grief and fear returns. It flows over my nakedness, and I shiver. Quick as I can, I wrap in the lavender goodness of the bedcover and roll on my side. The walls of the room close in, and I shiver some more. I curl up tight and the warm flow of tears comes again. Are they for Grandma Pat, or are they for me, the scared-silly me?

When I wake up, it is dark outside. Drool drips from my

mouth as I roll over to confirm the hour. I hold the covers close around me and consider the loud growl coming from my belly. It has been hours, all day, in fact since I last ate anything. Not since our breakfast near Pasaia Bay—a lifetime ago.

The thought of the city outside pulls at my guts; neck and jaw muscles tighten. I will stay in for the night. With my smartphone, I make an online order for pizza delivery. I didn't have a smartphone until last year, yet here I am ordering pizza delivery in a foreign country with the device. Things change.

What shall I do while I wait? I glance around the room. My attention falls on the two backpacks: mine, the bright blue one, and Grandma Pat's, a faded orange. Inside hers are the pages from Georgia's journal. Those "private things" call to me. What better way than to sit quietly—put on some clothes—eat pizza, and read their story? *Sorry, Grandma Pat.*

Dressed and cross-legged on the bed, I page through the hand-written diary. They had slept on a beach in France, hitchhiked here and there, visited old palaces, ancient churches, and gladiator arenas. How did Georgia know of such things? I wouldn't know about these places.

The smell of pizza arrives ahead of it. The woman delivering it sets the box on the chest of drawers and happily accepts the tip I offer to her. She looks to the pizza box and nods in appreciation of a girl-night in, probably wishing she could do the same, or join me.

Mrs. Ortiz, I assume, stops at the door as the delivery woman leaves. A very pretty lady, Mrs. Ortiz has long, dark hair and broad hips, and is slightly taller than her husband. If Paolo is her husband. In broken English and with a motherly nature, she asks if I need anything. I assure her I'll be fine. I turn aside to show her the pizza box, then smile. She understands. Women know about things, about situations. Father Ernesto is the only man I have met who comes close to that sort of intuition. The thought of him warms me, but hunger takes over.

I set the pizza box on a folded towel on the bed and pick up the lid. The sight makes my stomach grumble like it has never had food before. Sitting beside my meal and taking a huge bite, I slide the journal to my side and resume reading.

I come to the part about a mansion where they had stayed with some girls, and I learn about my grandmother and a musician named François. I feel like I'm doing something wrong. *Sorry, Grandma Pat, sorry for reading your secrets.*

Finished with this part of the journal I pull my phone closer. I put my mind to work on the near future, the Camino.

To successfully complete my trek to Santiago I need to plan. I love to plan. I have some cash in my pocket and Grandma Pat's wallet has more. There's Grandma Pat's debit card, too. I've used it before and know the PIN. I'll get euros from an ATM when I need more. My passport and the information for my flight home are in my backpack. And I have my phone. With it, I can email Tilly, or I can text or call my cousin Lou.

Perfectly timed, the notification of an email from Lou pops up on the screen. It's her mother's itinerary and flight number. In three days, Tilly will arrive in San Sebastián. I have to take the bus to collect her at the airport and bring her back into the city. *Dammit.*

San Sebastián, Spain
July 31, 1982
It has been two weeks, and I've saved up a few pesetas. San Sebastián, the beaches, the people—even the reserved Basque people—are great, but I should move on before too long. I talked with Mother last night. Thinking of starting to walk the Camino, I asked her about my wayward father, trying to find some clues of his whereabouts. She changed the subject, telling me about Pat's choice of college.

From Georgia's Travel Journal

SIX

San Sebastián, October 4, 2019

Tilly is the last person off the plane. It's just like her to drag out the process. She probably waited for every last passenger to offload, all to piss me off. Her wide, short frame waddles down the stairs to the tarmac and she shuffles her way to the terminal —through the same glass doors Grandma Pat and I had walked through less than a week ago. She drags a carry-on suitcase behind her. I wait to greet her on my side of the security checkpoint.

She has a look on her face. The usual one, like everything wrong in her life is my fault. Like I dragged her sister to Spain just for her to die here and make life more difficult for poor Tilly. I smile as cheerfully as possible. But I see it; here comes the storm.

"Where's my sister? Where the hell is this city you told me about? What's it called, San What? There's nothing here, nothing but this Podunk airport," she scoffs at me, as she waves her little hand around in the air like she's shooing away a bug.

I ignore her questions. "Did you make your connections all right? Did you check a bag?" Like all of a sudden I'm a seasoned traveler. Tilly looks me up and down. She has aged in the time since I last saw her. Pale and tired looking, dark bags hang under her eyes.

"Well . . .," she blows it out like it's the longest word in the English language, then goes on. "I only have this carry-on bag. I'm not staying here long. No longer than necessary. We will get you home, get Pat home so fast it'll—"

"I'm not going back with you, Aunt Tilly." I'm sure this news shocks her, but I need to get this over with. "I'm going to walk the Camino de Santiago for my grandmother," I say, then as an afterthought, "And hopefully find out what happened to your father."

She stops dead in her tracks. "The hell you will. You get me into this goddamn mess and then want me to take her home by myself. And that old man, who cares about him? He left me. Left me before I was even born. Up and went away. Probably dead by now."

I sense the hurt, her pain, but turn, step in close, and look down into her round, sad face. "It was her dying wish. I made a promise to my grandmother," I lie. I'm a liar. Well, not normally, other than telling people I'm an orphan so I don't have to explain my parents. I hate lying. But right now, I'm a liar, and lying is the best strategy I could invent.

She studies me again, sizing me up. Her appraisal means nothing to me.

Before she can get out another word, I move to phase two: "The bus to the city will show up in a few minutes. We should go and wait for it." I take her suitcase and steer her and her boggled expression out into the sunlight. "The bus stop isn't far, just across this parking lot."

The twenty-minute ride into the city is the longest ever. Tilly whines in my ear the whole time. Thankfully, we are well away from the few other passengers on the bus. All I can think about—as I ignore my grandmother's sister and her endless whimpering—are my last few days in San Sebastián. During my time here, I have adjusted to the noise, the buses flying by, the smells of sea and food and human beings. But I can't wait to leave this city, to get back on the trail and do nothing but walk, eat, sleep, and repeat. That's what Grandma Pat said we would do, and what Georgia had started telling her about in those journal pages.

Even though I didn't tell Tilly the truth, I know Grandma Pat would want me to finish what we had set out to do, to walk to Santiago de Compostela. Grandma Pat and I had walked the trail together for less than two days before she died. She taught me, or we taught each other, how uncomplicated it is to walk the Camino. And how beautiful, too. All I needed was a plan.

The night before, I read from Georgia's journal pages, seeking information. Next day, I sat on a park bench, people going about their business around me, and I sketched a plan for my first weeks on the trail. Gathering information from my grandmother's guidebook and my phone app, I could see the next town to stay for the night, where to buy what I needed, and the next village, and then the next.

Looking out the window of the bus as we enter San Sebastián —and wanting nothing more than to forget what has happened —Tilly's words finally penetrate, waking me from my trance. They stab at my brain like needles; in, then out, they go. In response to this, my body gives a slight shudder.

"Are you listening to me, Summer *Darling?*"

The emphasis to my surname is meant to aggravate me. It

works. "Look, *Aunt Tilly*, I didn't make your sister come here. It was her choice. Walking the Camino was her idea. And she wanted—"

"It most certainly was not her idea. That was all Georgia's doing. Our sister would traipse her skinny ass all over the goddamn globe and write us from who knows where. She put ideas in Patricia's head. Foolish ideas. Ideas like walking five hundred miles across the whole of Spain, for Pete's sake. I mean, who the hell does that sort of thing?"

"Three-hundred thousand people," I say with no more emphasis than needed. "Every year. Even more during Holy Years."

Thick blotches cover my great-aunt's neck and face, so bright she shines like a red disco ball. I notice, too, her eyes are bloodshot, pulsing. Tired from travel, the stress? *God, I hope she doesn't have a heart attack and die on me. Dammit, that's all I need. How would I explain it to the* policía *if she died? They'd throw me in jail for sure. Even Father Ernesto and his friends would find it impossible to get me out.*

I slump down in my seat, coming to eye level with her. "We shouldn't get upset with each other. Grandma Pat wouldn't want us arguing. She would say something like, 'We're all family, let's get along,' and we should." Complete horse manure, I know. Grandma Pat would want to choke the crap out of her sister right this minute—like I do.

She melts, the splotches beginning to fade. "Should have brought Louise with me; would have if she'd had a passport. I don't know what the hell I'm doing. I love my baby girl so much. She's better at this sort of mess, smarter. You are too." She lets it all go and starts crying. Every scrap of energy she had after her travels and her useless complaining melts away. I reach around her and pull her round, quivering body into mine.

The bus drops us at the train station across the river from the street leading to the Pensión Ortiz. Suspecting it's too much of a walk for Tilly, I guide her to a taxi. Paolo greets us at the check-in counter. I had reserved a room for Tilly after confirming her flight information. I get her settled and go to my room.

As I shed the day and Tilly's negativity, I dig out my phone to check for emails and texts from home. There's a text from Lou. She says another package has arrived for Grandma Pat from Spain. She wants to know if she should open it. I text a reply as fast as my thin fingers will work.

YES, OF COURSE

I wait. And wait.

Finally, her text arrives.

Opening now

I wait some more.

More of the journal

And a note

My fingers go to work.

WHAT DOES IT SAY?

I know Lou doesn't like all caps, but I can't help it.

Aún queda más por aprender. (There is still more to learn.)

What does it mean?

CAN YOU SCAN ALL AND EMAIL TO ME???

I wait and wait. When the pages finally show up in my inbox I start reading immediately. There are more than twenty of Georgia's lovely hand-written pages and the scribbled note.

On the first pages of this set, I read Georgia learned her father planned to walk and work his way along the Camino Francés, a different Camino route, inland from the north coast. He went to the city of Pamplona to start there. Georgia followed him. I have a lot to figure out if I'm going to follow her. This is going to be a long night, tomorrow an even longer day.

In the morning, Tilly and I meet for breakfast. Neither of us says much. Later, I ask Paolo to call us a taxi. The mortuary is several blocks away.

We enter the cold place and find the correct office and people we should talk with.

"Holy hell, that's a lot of money," Tilly erupts after I do the currency conversion with an app on my phone and relay the information to her. "We don't have the kind of money you are talking about. What are we supposed to do now? We want to take my sister home, dammit, not buy this whole country."

"Aunt Tilly, we—"

"Seriously?" she nearly shouts at the men.

"Grandma Pat had—"

Tilly steps sideways in front of me, quieting me. "You cannot expect this from us," Tilly says and gets closer to the men, gesticulating and repeating herself.

I tried, Aunt Tilly. I tried.

The men talk and show each other pieces of paper. They're waiting for this mad woman before them to run out of steam.

To one man, then another, she blazes about the costs and the time it will take to ready Grandma Pat for the flight home. Should I let her go on with this pathetic rant? Her objections go nowhere. The men remain calm, composed. She continues. I have visions of Tilly being arrested and hauled off to jail.

Finally, "Señora, señora, por favor, tranquile, please calm yourself," says the man in charge of processing my grandmother's body. The cops released Grandma Pat's body to the mortuary, but they need papers signed and want money before they will do whatever ghastly procedures they follow.

The corners of Tilly's mouth twitch with agitation. I feel sorry for these men. They have their jobs to get on with.

"She . . .," I circle Tilly and slip in between the warring factions.

Tilly clamps her mouth shut, crosses her arms across her chest, and stares at me. She puffs up like an inflating balloon about to burst.

I have a paper in my hands and make sure they all see it. "My Grandma Pat had travel insurance. The policy number and contact information are on this," I say and look to each of them. "I had copies made yesterday." I hand the pages over.

My aunt lets her arms drop, balls her fists, and steps close to me. I think she would attack me if we were alone.

Rodolfo says, "We go now, yes?" I could hug him.

"Mr. Ricado, please contact the insurance company, a European company. If you have questions for us, please call my aunt's phone number. You have it, yes?"

"Sí, señorita, sí," he says after his assistant shows him the phone number in a green file folder now bursting with pages. Mr. Ricado is a tall, handsome man with white hair, his assistant short and round. I can only imagine they have done this same thing too many times before, have had to ease the hysterics of family members of other deceased foreigners. They will embalm my grandmother's body, which sounds horrid. Then they will place her in a zinc-lined coffin and seal it. The proper person or persons have to sign off at every step in the process.

All of this, the paperwork, the police, the people at the mortuary, the constant conflict with my grandmother's sister has given me a pounding headache. Keeping Tilly under some form of control, doing the research and making sure we have everything these people need, and checking on flights for Grandma Pat's body and Tilly's return to San Diego has kept me distracted. But I'm desperate to put on my backpack and walk, to get away from people, to get out of the city, to stroll in peace again.

Before Grandma Pat saved me from them, I lived in the woods in the place my parents called home. Even when I was younger, I could wander away from the group of shacks they all called "The Camp." There, wandering among gargantuan cedars and fir trees was the most peaceful place to hang out. I could absorb my surroundings. A soft blanket of fir needles and cedar fans coated the forest floor and the scent of the forest flushed away any concerns I had for my life with the bickering, so-called adults. Little Michael and I were always as happy to steal away from the adults as they were for us to do so. He was a skinny, towheaded boy of seven or eight when we moved there. Few ever cared to remember his age.

Michael would follow me around most places I went. He was lonely. He needed someone with functioning brain cells as much as I did. But oftentimes I wanted to go off by myself to smell the woods and feel the earth beneath me. I would pick up duff from the forest floor and draw in its layers of musty aromas. In those quiet moments, Michael would startle me, frozen in place, his eyes locked on me, a curious, what-is-she-doing? look on his face. He often scared me this way. He was difficult to read in those moments, sort of creepy looking. As we grew up, however, we did become friends. What choice did we have?

As I often do, I wonder about Michael. Did his grandmother finally come for him? I can only hope. He looked so desperate, so miserable when we pulled away in Grandma Pat's car, me looking out the passenger-side window, a palm flat on the glass, nearly as unhappy. I left the camp behind and glad of it. But I was also leaving my parents, goofy as they were, and abandoning poor Michael.

Trying to forget that traumatic day, remembering the countryside and Mother Nature's perfume, I realize Spain has a lot of nature yet for me to enjoy.

I need to finish up here. I also need to call Father Ernesto and tell him about my plans for the Camino Francés. By now, I've read quite a lot about the Camino from France, the route most pilgrims take to Santiago. He will want—or need—to know my plans.

As our taxi drives us the few blocks to the Pensión Ortiz, Tilly starts at me again. "You will go home with me, Summer. Enough of this craziness about you wandering off on your own. That was Georgia's idea, and your grandmother's silliness. You are too young. You must come home with me, you hear?" Hearing no response from me, she goes on, "I am your guardian now. You are my responsibility."

Tilly responsible for me? I shudder at the thought and continue to gaze out the window, out to the city environment. My backpack is ready to go. It has been packed and repacked a dozen times. The only extra weight I will carry are the journal pages in their protective sleeve and Grandma Pat's wallet and notebook.

"You are not listening to me. But you will go home with me. You have to, you just have to, Summer."

I let out a long sigh.

She pleads . . . and cries again. I do sort of feel bad. We have argued this point for two days now. But I desperately want to walk for my Grandma Pat. All the way to Santiago. Tilly wriggles around to look straight at me.

"I will tell the police. They will put your ass on that damn plane with me," she bawls.

Turning from the window I see her, the pouty lips, and puffy eyes. "I will reschedule my flight and get a seat on the same plane as you and Grandma Pat." *Liar.*

San Sebastián, Spain
August 1, 1982
Well, it's time to leave this beautiful city; I need to start my Camino. The secretary at the cathedral found someone to send her a pilgrim credential for me to use as I walk across Spain. My sister simply could not imagine doing such a thing. I'm super excited about the proposition. More churches and cathedrals. More beautiful Spanish men, too.

From Georgia's Travel Journal

SEVEN

San Sebastián, October 7, 2019

As dawn breaks, the transport van pulls away. My guts are in knots. Tilly looks miserable. Grandma Pat's coffin, sitting on a simple aluminum bier, waits outside of the terminal, her backpack on a tray underneath, both lonely and sad. The storms passed by this morning, two of them. All outdoors dribbles wet from last night's showers. And Tilly has had her eruption of tears and ranting and belittling me. Was it the last Tilly-storm? No. I know better.

Has everything been done properly for Grandma Pat? We will soon find out. I may feel better once she goes on board the plane, which has yet to arrive. At least, I hope so.

Tilly and I are in the little airport's only café, La Pausa. She sits at a table in one corner of the room cradling a steaming cup of coffee close to her nose. Looking out the floor-to-ceiling windows I can see the white coffin we chose for Grandma Pat yesterday. Tilly called it, "Simple yet elegant." Those were the nicest words I think she has ever said.

Beyond this sad view, I can see dark, gray clouds resting on the peaks of the Pyrenees. Feeling almost poetic—another new experience for me—the scene sort of represents how life seems at this moment: a gray asphalt foundation with people shuffling about, doing what they do; green, everywhere green, moist, and refreshed, the hope of a new day blooming; and gray, brooding clouds framing the top like the storm which has passed and a forecast of others to come.

With a deep breath, I draw in what I need and expel what I don't want or don't need. I don't need Tilly's negativity, but I most certainly need Grandma Pat's stubbornness and her drive.

The ground crew starts fussing about; the morning flight from Madrid is coming in to land. I take in more of the Spanish air—I cannot draw it in deep enough—and then let it go.

The airplane settles to a stop. Passengers climb down the stairs and walk across the tarmac. A small crew goes to work unloading baggage. The same men ready the plane for its departure and quickly load Grandma Pat's casket. A dark cloud skulks past. I know how it feels.

As soon as I lift my backpack from the floor, Tilly gets up and comes to my side. "Time to go?"

"Yeah, sure." Not thinking it possible, my gut tightens even more. "We need to get through security."

It's our turn, Tilly's turn. She steps up to the officer checking passports and boarding passes. Once he has cleared her, she steps through a simple gate. Immediately, another officer waves her forward to pass though the airport's single metal detector. She hesitates. He quickly waves his hand again, drawing her forward with his gesture. Once through the machine, she turns back expecting to see me right behind her. She's standing sideways and looking over her shoulder. I'm not there and I see her body go rigid. She stretches as tall as she can and searches for me.

Before reaching passport check, I stepped out of line, letting other passengers pass me by. Through the distance between Tilly and me, I see it penetrate. Her eyes grow wide and fill with fire. She finds me.

She's about to explode. Having expected this moment for so long, I relax, resigned to the torrent I expect any second now. She will have her say—loud as it may be—and I will go. My only worry: will she keel over, right there on the spot. God, I hope not. I can only have hope.

Tilly spins and faces me. "You planned this all along, didn't you, you little turd," she yells above the din of voices and machines. The security officers stop in place, raised hands, palms facing out, holding the next passengers in the line. They turn toward Tilly, serious scowls on every face.

Tilly glances over her shoulder to the airplane. She spins around and starts to return the way she came. An officer steps directly in front of her, stopping her. She glowers at me, then for a long moment again stares at the airplane on the tarmac. She sways in both directions and eases in my direction.

The officer, his hands still in the air, glares at my great-aunt. He is tall, mostly thin, with a pillowy thickness above his belt.

When she looks for me again, I am gone, lost among the crowd.

I walk back to the café, hoping Tilly goes with her sister. At the glass wall again, I watch as Tilly, the closest family I have, other than my cousin Lou, walk away from me, out there on a patch of asphalt in a little airport in a sweet-smelling corner of Spain. She and the other passengers climb into the airplane. Tilly never looks back.

The warm liquid returns from nowhere; tears burn a path

down my face and drip on the floor. I turn away, having a bus to catch to San Sebastián, and one last stop to visit a friend.

Father Ernesto comes out of his cathedral to meet me. Ever entering that building again, the place where Grandma Pat took her last breath, seems inconceivable to me. Father Ernesto understands and walks toward the bench where I sit. He doesn't question my feelings or ridicule me like Tilly would. He simply smiles his soft smile and sits down beside me.

He has on the same brown robe, the same worn leather belt around his middle. For the first time I notice he wears slacks and simple leather sandals under his robe.

"You seem more at ease today, Summer. Are you ready to continue your journey?"

"Yes, Father. But I wanted to thank you for your help with . . . with everything."

"You do not need to thank me. You know Whom I think you should thank. But I understand your feelings in such regard, so I leave you to discover Him on your own."

I look to his kind face and absorb his words. "I should get going, Father."

"You are very young, but wiser than your years, my child. Summer. The Camino will challenge you and provide for you. Be open to its glory and vigilant for your safety."

Father Ernesto digs around under his robe again and pulls out a piece of folded paper. He hands it to me. I unfold the page. There's a name and a phone number on it. The friend in Pamplona he had mentioned before, when I called to tell him of the new pages from Georgia's journal. "When you arrive in this city, please call Father Emil, he will help you find a place for the night, or for as long as you need.

And Father Emil will call his friend in San Sebastián and let him know how I am doing. I look to the padre with a knowing smile. He averts his eyes from my gaze.

With the grace of a swan, he rises from the bench and reaches down with his slender arms and vein-streaked hands to take mine in his.

I stand and want to wrap my arms around this man, want to give him a quick hug. I've never been one to like hugs and feel surprised by this urge. Surprised by my approach, he stiffens, standing straight and severe. I pull back from the forward lean and feel a flush of heat roll up my neck. He smiles softly and turns back to his gothic cathedral.

I lift my backpack onto my shoulders, buckle and tighten the straps, and begin walking toward the beach.

Not since my grandmother's last day have I seen this wide curved stretch of sand. At a crosswalk, I follow nicely dressed businesspeople to a wide path above the beach. Only a few people walk their dogs on the beach beside the flat waters of the bay. I turn left and, in a few seconds, find the first yellow arrow in nearly a week, a splash of paint on a light pole pointing west. The sight of it floods me with a warm happiness—and trepidation, I've got to admit. As I walk on, what has happened in recent days replays in my mind. It seems like forever ago that we walked into this city. I have learned so much, things I had no need for not long ago. So many good people have come into my life since. Sure, there was Tilly—now grumbling to another poor soul where she's seated on an airplane—and there were a few irritating bureaucrats to deal with in the process. But there were Father Ernesto and Rudolfo, Paolo and his lovely wife, Annette, and others. All such kind people.

For now, I will set these memories aside, and walk on. Walk and pull thick, moist air deep into my lungs.

It's hard to explain to most people my love for solitude and nature, and the struggle I feel when in crowds and around stupid people. Perhaps feeling that way about some people has nothing to do with liking solitude. It could indicate another trait all together. Or perhaps Grandma Pat influenced me. Her customers came first—until they crossed a line.

Perhaps, too, it was my previous life. When I was about seven years old, there was a raid of our camp near some apple orchards. Police and federal agents stormed the place, arresting several of my parents' friends. How my parents avoided arrest, I'll never know. I was in the orchard, under my favorite tree, or they might have taken me away. I couldn't decide afterward if it would have been a bad thing or not. It's hard, too, loving your parents and hating them at the same time.

People pass me by, walking their dogs or talking with colleagues. Couples arm in arm. But no backpack-adorned pilgrims with their trekking poles push themselves up the paved path. I have missed the morning's pilgrim rush out of San Sebastián.

More yellow arrows guide me up and out of the city and onto a hillside covered with eucalyptus trees, their leaves rattling against each other in a slight breeze. Climbing, my legs are happy with the activity, heart and lungs pleased with the work. It's like they are purring. It's my mind, though, that feels the happiest. I know where to stop for the night, where to find a bed and something to eat. So, for now, I walk.

I feel my grandmother here, still my tour guide, this time from behind, over one shoulder. It's a feeling, a warmth, a knowing that her presence stays with me.

The Camino del Norte is ours for a while.

California can wait for me. Lou can wait until I have finished this walk across Spain for my Grandma Pat.

Zarautz, Spain
August 2, 1982

It's only day two. I have met some pilgrims already. I asked my questions, learning the ropes. Getting up early may be a problem, though. I'm not accustomed to waking before the sun and starting to walk at dawn.

From Georgia's Travel Journal

EIGHT

Orio, October 8, 2019

It's light outside. I meant to leave early this morning, beat other pilgrims to the trail and the day. But I didn't sleep well last night. It was too quiet, nothing to distract me from my busy mind. The little town of Orio, at the mouth of a river and a port, is sleepy at best, boring really. Did my time in San Sebastián civilize me? Oh, I hope not.

I'm a teenager; I should sleep until noon. But I seldom do. I'm not normal. Lou has said this, while we laugh about it. Mornings have been my sanctuary since I can remember. The early hours of daylight in camp were mine to explore and find peace. I would find my parents curled up together on a broken-down couch beside a smoldering campfire, other couples nearby, some lying in the dirt. Beer cans and bottles always strewn around, remnants of another all-nighter. I often cleaned up their messes. Even throwing bottles into a basket to haul to a recycling bin I built by the maintenance shack didn't wake those supposed adults.

Daylight didn't wake me this morning—an ugly blister had the pleasure. The raw flesh of my angry toe snagged in the bedsheets and brought me to life with a stab of searing pain.

Now my foot soaks in the tub, and I'm searching through my blister kit for something to protect the wounded digit from today's many miles. The Camino app says it's a twenty-mile trek to Deba, where I plan to stay tonight. I come across a roll of white tape my grandmother had thrown into my kit. She knew about blisters. *Ampollas,* the Spanish call them.

After drying my foot and assessing the loose dermal layer, I wrap the toe with a layer of tape. Should I have put something between the tape and my skin? I didn't. I'll hope for the best. I have read through my favored anatomy textbook a few times. I remember much of it. But the knowledge gained there does not help much with my damaged anatomy.

I hope to sleep better tonight. I'm not sure what it was last night that kept me up. Was it the thought of a full day on the Camino del Norte without my grandmother? Was it Georgia's journal? Again, I read through the pages I have, bouncing around from place to place, story to story. She and my Grandma Pat had some adventures as they hitchhiked and rode trains and buses around southern France, into Andorra—a country I had never heard of before last night—and into Spain.

First time through, I read Georgia's words in proper order. Now I pick her story up wherever. I might read about them skinny-dipping with new friends in France or being interrogated at a border crossing. They did have some episodes (Georgia's word) their mother would not have approved of.

Do I approve of them? Does it matter if I do or not?

Why in hell am I brooding this morning? That's what Grandma Pat called it when I got quiet. She also called my brooding, navel-gazing. *Ick.* I'm alone, with time to think. Thinking too much. But why? Do I avoid the real questions: Why am I here? Why am I doing this alone? Why didn't I return to California with Aunt Tilly?

There's a simple answer: *Because, we finish what we start.*

It's time for me to go. I ease my shoes on and tie the laces, then pick up my backpack.

I step out of the pensión and into a chill morning air with my breakfast, a granola bar, clamped between my teeth. I weave down a narrow sidewalk, trying to heft the backpack onto my shoulders. As it sets onto sore muscles I groan like an old man, nearly dropping my breakfast. I'm leaving town, passing humble homes and shops made of stone. The streets are still quiet. A woman and her dog walk with purpose in my direction, then turn down a side street. I guess off to buy fresh bread at the bakery or down to the marina to get some fish. But who knows? Sturdy build, in plain clothes, the woman wears a tattered apron covering her from chest to kneecaps. The scruffy dog rushes ahead. Apparently, he knows their familiar destination.

The sky ripples with puffy clouds. A dark one rolls in, and large raindrops begin to fall in a steady rhythm. A tap, tap of rain beats out a tune on rooftops and my head. My thoughts run from painful toe to wet ball cap. As I consider stopping for my raincoat, the rain ceases. Everything is damp and dark.

Before I can regain my Camino stride, Georgia's words return. Grandma Pat was young once. She had experiences. She wasn't like Georgia, who would rush into an encounter with a boy simply to experience someone different. But, if I believe what her sister wrote, my grandmother did spend the night with a man at a chateau in France. Growing up where I did, I saw men and women rushing off to a cabin or into the forest for their own experiences. And there was Paul, the camp's leader, my father's friend.

Paul was always after one woman or another, no matter if they were married or not. I think my mother was the only one he never slept with. Well, her, and me. When my parents had enough of Paul cozying up to me, "grooming" me Laura called it, they called Grandma Pat. The thought sends a shiver from my wet, cap-covered head to my angry and blistered toe. I'm growing up, but sex and love, it all seems so complicated. I crave simple things; I'll stick to books and Georgia's stories. *Will we receive more from her soon?*

I'm at the edge of town now. A tongue of fog reaches upriver, nearly to town, licking at ships tied at port. The trail turns upward, away from the water. There are other pilgrims ahead of me. We climb through the rolling terrain of pastures and vineyards. The tape around my toe wriggles from its place. The blister pinches occasionally, which sends a stabbing pain through my foot. Is it bleeding? *If it is, what should I do about it, Grandma Pat?*

She doesn't bother to answer my question, but her presence comforts me as we make our way along this easy path. If she could, she'd say something like, *figure it out*. Or her favorite, *Get on with it, girl.*

But what? What do I need to learn or do to get through today, to get through tomorrow, to arrive in Santiago in time for my flight home?

Deba, Spain
August 3, 1982

They say this route has more climbing than others, much more in the days and weeks ahead. And I'm already slowing down. This town is wonderful, quaint. I've been told there is a nice beach at the mouth of the Deba River. I could check it out tomorrow.

From Georgia's Travel Journal

<u>NINE</u>

Zarautz, October 8, 2019

Trying to boost my confidence, I stroll into the next seaside town like I have done this a hundred times before. Neat and tidy apartment buildings line the roadway beside a sandy beach. Offshore, a few surfers wait for the very best waves. The rich fragrance of fresh brewed coffee claws at me as I pass a café on the edge of town. I prefer to drink tea, but the aroma of coffee as it flows through my olfactory system always perks me up. I can see a café ahead. I could stop.

Three pilgrims, their packs lying under a table outside the café, sip from tiny cups and chat. They wave a greeting in my direction.

I feel my heart rate jump and shoulders scrunch toward my ears, and I ease through any interest in coffee or tea. In another moment I have left the town behind.

Quickly, I come to a route choice: follow the coast road along a wide promenade or the trail into the hills above the sea?

Thinking of the stupid blister on my toe, I decide on the coast route.

Waves slop onto the rocky shore and salty mist drifts over me as I walk this path for another pair of miles and until I come to another town. I can see backpack-adorned hikers well ahead. Also, here and there are elderly men with simple canes strolling close to the railing at the edge of the path and near the sea. Perhaps they are retired fishermen who cannot stray far from their former workplace. They tip their hats, dipping the bill in an old-fashioned way. Some say mashed or shortened greetings in Spanish. *"Buendía,"* or simply *"Día."* It's so quaint.

Why did I avoid those people in the last village? Yes, I prefer solitude, so much of my life has been that way. But while working for Grandma Pat at the café, talking with people, it got a little easier for me. Well, some of the time. Here now, the feeling is different, easy. Will I learn to like people, care about them?

After another small town, the Camino route climbs into beautiful, glistening green countryside, so completely different from home this time of year. And I love this, love the moist air and stunning surroundings.

Fixed on this scene, I had not noticed two trekkers ahead of me. Too close to avoid them, I speed up to pass. One of them, a man, says, *"Buen Camino."*

In a muted and rushed squeak, I return the greeting. To say "Good Way" in Spanish is the traditional greeting of pilgrims. I had read about this and have heard it said a few times since our start, but this is the first time I have uttered the words myself. I'm embarrassed by my clumsy response and feel a flush run up my face like a red tide.

Now, higher, and farther inland, the Camino traverses an exposed ridge and droopy rain clouds skirt close by. I am wet from perspiring and the soft drizzle the clouds share refreshes me. I keep everything in a dry bag inside my pack. As the rain stops, I come to a vacant campground with a few picnic tables under leafy mulberry trees, a perfect spot for a quick snack. I select a picnic table for my break. I set my pack on the bench and sit beside it on top of the table, a grand view in front of me. Last night, with this moment in mind, I was lucky enough to find some goodies in a market. I spread a super ripe, nutty smelling avocado over rustic bread made from course-milled flour. My mouth waters as I admire the meal in my hand.

"Buen Camino."

I jerk in surprise; I hadn't heard him coming. He smiles at my alarmed reaction. He's there, then gone, moving out of sight as the trail drops and rounds a corner. The energy of those few seconds collapses and again I have this peaceful place to myself.

As I stand to reload my things, pain rockets from my foot, my old buddy, a blasted blister. I press the toe of my shoe into the ground and gently wriggle my foot, hoping to reposition the tape I had wrapped it with earlier. It seems to work, and the pain subsides. I set my pack on its home, buckle up, and begin an afternoon of strolling through these hills made especially for me.

I find this peaceful, this walk, stroll, trek, saunter. As soon as the path drops into a vale, it flattens, then goes upward, and continues this cycle at the next ridge. At each transition it feels like someone has shot me in the foot. With my toe-tap-wriggle move, I reposition the tape holding the blister together. At least I hope it's holding the blister together. Blood would make this a bad day.

Ahead of me now, and along a blacktop lane, there's a village and its lone church steeple. An older woman pilgrim—*peregrina*, if I remember correctly—is coming toward me, which seems odd. She moves slowly, trekking poles far out to her sides. Her backpack looks heavy. The sun has appeared, shining brightly on our stretch of road and the sloping, brilliantly green terrain.

As we come close, she stops. "Are you okay, dear?"

"I, uh. . ." It takes me a second to realize I'm limping down this hill. "Oh, yes, I'm fine."

"A new blister?"

"Not new. I'll do something with it this evening," I say, while hedging to continue walking.

"We could look at it now. . ." As I come closer, she looks into my eyes. "I have dealt with a few of those wicked buggers myself."

I stop before her and ponder my feet—and her suggestion.

"It wouldn't take long," she says.

I look up and see her kindly expression. Should I? "I taped it this morning. The bandage gets out of place sometimes."

"Where are you from, sweetie?"

"California."

"Ah, I see. I'm from Ohio. I finished in Santiago and liked this part of Spain so much I decided to walk the Norte again, this time in the other direction."

The idea doesn't make any sense to me.

"Are you sure about your foot?" She looks from my face to the foot and back. I hesitate. Should I deal with it? "Are you by yourself?"

"Yes."

"You seem kind of young for an American girl. On her own, I mean," she says.

"I'm eighteen," I say as confidently as possible. I don't let it linger, though. "I don't have far to Deba. I can deal with it then, it's only one toe." She seems torn by my reluctance. So am I. She stands there, a thin smile on her lips. Apparently hoping I'll change my mind. Which makes up my mind. I stand there looking back at her with a similar smile. I concentrate on slowing the work my lungs do, calming my heart rate.

"Well, Buen Camino, to you," she finally says as she begins

her slow, purposeful plod up the hill. "Take care of your foot, soon as you can."

After a moment, I realize I'm not moving, just thinking about my dumb toe. I try to let it go and start walking again. I do limp, but it's not too bad. Winding through the village, I stop to take a picture of the little church, then continue, returning to a mix of crops and oak forests.

My mind wanders as I ignore the pain in my foot that comes and goes. I recall bits of Aunt Georgia's journal that I have read. Grandma Pat, before they separated that summer in 1982, had asked Georgia if she would search for their father. Georgia had been telling Grandma Pat about the Camino de Santiago. The idea of going on pilgrimage had come up many times during their weeks traveling Europe together. Georgia had met a woman planning to walk to Santiago. Georgia wanted a new adventure, and her sister Pat had posed an interesting question about their father. Would she find him, could she find him as she walked across Spain?

Deba, Spain
August 4, 1982
I don't know if it's a thing, or even appropriate for a pilgrim, but I'm calling this a rest day. Beach, here I come.

From Georgia's Travel Journal

TEN

Deba, October 8, 2019

I slip from a forest and toward the town of Deba. More than a seaside village, but less than a port city, the town below fills a narrow river valley. Passing newer apartment buildings, the Camino route begins to descend by stairway down into the center of town. My toe really makes me mad. I'm sure it's bleeding by now.

Not far away, I see a boy with dark skin and a large backpack under a dark blue poncho. It had rained a few drops earlier, up in the hills, but I hadn't bothered with rain gear. The very top of his head is covered with standing curls dyed bright yellowish orange. He looks like a big blue marshmallow skewered by a long matchstick just set on fire.

He looks lost, confused. He glances at his smartphone, looks up, turns this way and that. He spies a woman walking his way along the narrow lane. He calls to her. I can only make out part of what he says, "looking for the all-pear-kay."

The woman indicates in perfect English she doesn't have the

time, she's in a hurry. She rushes to her car, slams the door, and buzzes away. I'm as surprised . . . as the matchstick is.

I'm near to him now. He turns to me and without hesitation says something similar about an albergue. I weed through his thick accented words.

"Yellow arrows point down the staircase over there," I say, pointing in their direction and resuming my stroll-limp toward the stairs and the center of town. He follows close behind, kind of too close. I speed up the best I can. On the stairs, keeping my toe pointed up, I step only on my heel. This doesn't do much good.

He says, "Which way I not know. I need find all-pear-kay."

Over the pain of my toe and through clenched teeth, I say, "You'll find the al-bear-gay down there, in the town." I wonder how this guy found his way this far along the Camino del Norte. "Are you looking for the municipal albergue?"

"Municipal, yes. Need find," he says.

I can't stand it anymore and stop before the next set of stairs to let him pass. He stops too. "Go ahead," I say with a wave.

"Which way I not know," he says again. I point down the stairway. He stands there. *Weirdo.*

I go ahead, as fast as I can manage.

The yellow arrows lead down and through a narrow alley before entering a plaza. I look for Matchstick. He is missing. Where in the hell did he go? I look around, turning full circle. He's gone. What's with that guy?

I see a market on the other side of the plaza, next to another splash of yellow and a sign indicating the direction of the municipal albergue. I hope he finds it.

After resupplying at the market, it's time for me to find the pensión where I plan to stay the night. A few blocks from the plaza I walk past the municipal albergue. There he is. Matchstick. He found it somehow; I'm not sure how.

He talks with a couple of women pilgrims as they wait at the front door. One presses an intercom button and speaks with someone inside. Matchstick comes close to the other woman. I see the same discomfort I felt earlier in her eyes and body language. I slink away, heading for my destination. Sorry to dump this lost soul on you, ladies. But it wasn't my doing. He seems confused, even when he knows where he is. I've seen that look before.

Little Michael, my friend at the camp in the forest, struggled to find his way—even in simple situations. There were no role models or teachers for him before we moved into the cabin across camp from where he and his useless parents lived. I say "useless" because they were always stoned. They made Michael but had no idea what to do with him afterward.

Like it knows we are close to the day's end, my toe screams even louder with each step. I limp, straight legged and heel down, across the main street in search of a place to sit down and take off my shoes.

In the entranceway of the establishment, a thin, pretty woman with shoulder-length dark hair leans against the doorframe. When she sees me coming and the pain I am in, she stands tall and a look of concern spreads across her soft features.

She moves aside to welcome me through the doorway. "Where have you come from today?"

"Orio," I say as I look around inside for a place to sit. I can only see doorways to other rooms, a few coat hooks, and a rack for shoes on one wall.

"Ah, many kilometers, many miles. You need to sit," she says and guides me into another room.

As I follow her, I ask, "Do you have a room for the night?"

"Yes, yes. First, let us look at your foot. I help many pilgrims with their many blisters."

In a flash, I sit down in her kitchen, my backpack leaned

against one wall. She gently bares my foot. I see blood. My head spins at the sight of raw flesh. The blister, as big as the toe, has burst open. Bright red blood and clear serum ooze from under a loose flap of gray necrotic epidermis.

Quickly, the owner of this place, Maria, has scissors, gauze, and tape at hand. She trims away the now-useless skin, then gives the site closer inspection and deftly trims some more. She stands and pulls a bottle of clear liquid from a shelf and returns. She moistens a cotton ball.

"This will hurt," she says, as she quickly dabs the alcohol on the wound. I don't have time to consider what is coming my way.

It hurts like hell, but only for a few moments.

As Maria leaves the wound to dry, she inspects my feet for other damage. Happy with her handiwork, she puts some padding under the big toe and tapes it solid. A couple of other red spots have formed, one on each heel. She puts tape over. "We let the tape set to your skin. Tomorrow, good to go," she says. "Are you alone tonight?"

"Yes." I don't bother to tell Maria I'm alone every night. This news doesn't seem to matter to Maria as much as the American woman earlier today.

"One room then. And supper? Tonight, beef stew, fresh baked bread, and dessert. Five euros."

I nod and add a happy smile. My stomach asks *when*? Soon, it hopes.

"Rest here while I check you in for the night," she says as she stands and walks away.

I am happy to sit for a while. I'll text Lou while I wait. I hope Tilly has calmed down by now.

I have never walked—or limped—this far in my short life. It feels good to have done so, and my toe is happier than half an hour ago. The farthest I ever walked before today was the few miles roundtrip to my secret swimming hole on the Olympic

Peninsula. I was always happy to get away from the adults, and the walk went by without a thought of how far it might be.

My mind comes back to Spain. I recall the strange boy I met outside of town. He found his albergue. What will his tomorrow look like, I wonder? I may run into him again. He is the youngest person I have seen so far during the start of my trek across Spain. I think of him as Matchstick, but I wonder what his real name is, and what his story is. We all have a story. Like my little friend Michael. Or me, if I'm honest with myself.

Why is life so complicated? The big fat question of the day.

Markina-Xemein, Spain
August 5, 1982
Staying tonight in the good-sized town surrounded by logging and rock quarries. Later, I'm meeting a few other pilgrims for dinner on the square.

From Georgia's Travel Journal

ELEVEN

Deba, October 9, 2019

Maria has breakfast set out. Toasted baguette, olive oil, and black tea lie on the small table before me. A coarse cotton cloth covers the table, a tattered lace around its edge. My stomach gurgles in anticipation. I cannot remember ever being so hungry. Daylight fills a window facing the main street. Trucks occasionally rumble past.

Maria enters from the kitchen. "How does your foot feel today, little one?" Though I am much taller than her, she has called me "little one" a few times now.

"It feels so much better this morning. Muchas gracias, Maria," I say as I happily dip a teabag into a steaming cup of water. "I have another long day planned."

"Do you walk to Bolibar today?"

"For the distance I want to average, I plan to stay at a monastery at Zenarruza, above Bolibar."

"Ah, yes," she says as she sits with me, a coffee with steamed milk in her hands. "A long, hard walk in the hills. But muy bonita, very pretty."

I have a hard time tearing myself away from the comfort of Maria's home, from the smell of coffee and something marvelous and savory smelling baking in the oven. This place is warm and cozy, inviting. It reminds me of Paolo and Annette at the Pensión Ortiz, and of the places Grandma Pat and Georgia had stayed. Georgia called them "boutique hotels."

I read a few pages of her journal last night before falling to sleep. I was so tired from the long day I didn't get far. I did learn that some of the men the sisters met during their trip were not good people. *Drug smugglers, Grandma Pat?*

After collecting my pack, I come back down the stairs, stop in the dining room, and say a quick goodbye. Other people are up now, and Maria rushes around the room. She slows for a moment to wish me a "Buen Camino," before I step out into a beautiful day.

The sun has not yet reached into the river valley, but the sky above is a bright clean blue.

I cross the river on a temporary platform above a broken-down bridge in desperate need of repair. At the other side, the path follows a paved road for a short while then ducks into the countryside. Abruptly, in a good way, I am back in nature. A familiar calm takes over. The route climbs from the valley, the warm feeling of my Grandma Pat shielding me like a protective bubble. Other hikers are ahead. I glance from one group to another, expecting to see Matchstick. *You gotta stop calling him that.*

Arrows direct us into a dark forest and the path steepens. Yesterday's strong legs are tired quadriceps today. For the first time I struggle to keep to my desired pace. The complaining muscles remind me of the poles strapped to my pack. I pull a toggle down, loosening a springy cord, and extract the bundle of carbon-fiber sticks. They are quick to pop into long shafts when I straighten them. I push off with one, then the other. In a few strides I wonder why I had not used them before now. Once out of the valley, I feast on the sun and celebrate in the shade as I return to a reasonable walking speed.

Rounding a steep corner, my head down, I sense something strange, like someone is watching me. I look up and glance left. Matchstick. He's there, just sitting there. He has perched himself on a rock wall, his backpack and poncho looking like when I first saw him above Deba. He stares at me with odd, intense eyes as I climb toward him.

I want to walk on and avoiding talking to him at all, but I stop and lean on my poles like I had seen my grandmother do. "Hello, again."

"Where you sleep the night?" he asks.

"Oh, a pensión not far from the albergue, a nice place," I say. As I mull over his tone of voice, I look to him, trying to read him, to understand this guy.

He sits there with a deep stare. Because I have seen it before, I suspect he is damaged by an unknown past. Unknown to me. Perhaps that's what makes humans interested in each other: We are all damaged somehow, have a story.

He slips from the rock wall and stands. "I go now. Go with you now, yes?" he says as he comes close to my side. Again, too close for my comfort.

"Yeah, sure. I wanted to get your name anyway. I have not met any others close to my age." We start walking, resuming the climb.

"I am Rond, from Norway, my home," he says.

I give him a long glance.

"My mother. . . she is from Africa," he says.

"Rond. That's an interesting name," I say, hoping for more. He says nothing but has his eyes on me. "My name is Summer. You know, like the season."

As our silence lingers, my heart rate raises, shoulder muscles tighten. Rond is not making it any easier. He's still too close to me as we walk. Will this be my Camino experience? Will we walk quietly in a tension-filled bubble for the next thirty days? How did I get Michael to talk with me at the camp in the forest? Questions.

Well at least I have a proper name for him.

The Camino climbs, flattens out for a while, then begins to roll up and down like it had yesterday. We hike through lush rolling fields, some with donkeys and cows, and past farmhouses with fruit trees and vegetable gardens, the last of the season's tomatoes ripening on the vine.

The beauty of this place, and the tension of walking with a strange man, has kept me from thinking about my feet. Which is a good thing. As we pass a nice, older home with a large garden behind a rock wall, I assess the blister Maria so helpfully bandaged for me. It and the few other hotspots feel pretty good, especially considering how my feet felt yesterday at this time.

Ahead of us walk the three pilgrims I saw having coffee in one of the villages yesterday. At least I think it's them.

Rond and I still don't say anything to one another. As we walk, stride for stride, we come to the other group, and I am drawn close to them but not quite into their sphere. Rond slides away from me, staying slightly away from the group.

"We waved to you in Zarautz, yesterday. We had stopped for coffee," says one of the women to me in accented English.

"Oh, yeah, sorry. I was trying to decide on coffee or not," I say, as if it's the whole truth.

"I am Sofia. She's Eugenia," says the first woman as she points to the tall, thin one with chestnut dreadlocks. "And Claudia," she says with a nod in the opposite direction. Small and spritely, Sofia has dark hair. Claudia is older, not exactly pretty, but elegant in a way, with square shoulders and a straight posture.

"My name is Summer. He is Rond," I say as I nod toward the blue marshmallow now walking ahead of us. Quickly, I add, "We met not far back."

He glances back with a thin-lipped smile. He remains quiet and stays at his steady pace. His trekking poles work back and forth under his big blue poncho, stabbing the gravel path as we go.

The women look at me. Timidly, I look into their eyes. Then we return our focus to the path.

As we trek up one hill and down another, I learn that these three women are from Germany but had not met until a few days ago. They are already comfortable friends. Rond walks a little faster than our covey, pulling away from us.

Sofia leans my way, "You met him today?"

"Well, no, yesterday, sort of," I say. "But we didn't introduce ourselves until this morning. He stayed in the municipal albergue. I stayed at a pensión across the road." They nod in acknowledgment.

As we hike along, Claudia steps into the gap between me and Sofia. "We saw him at the muni last night, Sof. He was the guy having trouble with the washing machine."

Sofia visibly flinches and turns to me. "Claudia has spent too much time in your America. She shortens people's names, a bad habit," she says, then glances at her new friend.

Claudia apologizes. "Sorry. Yes, bad habit. Do you remember him from last night, Sofia?"

I worry Rond will hear our conversation. Our pace slows.

Sofia shakes her head. Eugenia joins in and says, "I remember him. He slept in the dorm upstairs. He's the guy who had a mouse climb into his pack. Everyone laughed. He thought they laughed at him. Someone else helped him though, and they took the mouse outside."

The slowed stride becomes our steady pace, for now. Rond is well ahead. Conversation turns to where each of us had started this journey and when we plan to arrive in Santiago, or not. Claudia has to leave the Norte in Gijon, three weeks from now, and return to her work. Sofia and Eugenia will continue trekking to Santiago but have no real timeline or constraints, it seems. I only tell them I will finish in Santiago by the 10th of November. I'll follow Georgia's journal, what I know of it, anyway. But I don't give out those details. Santander and the bus I will take to Pamplona are more than a week away.

Up ahead, Rond stops at a crest in our path. He turns and casts a little wave toward us. He stands there for a moment longer, staring. I can feel the others stiffen at his gaze. I decide to interpret his hand wave as a sign he's okay, only shy. If so, I totally get it.

He turns and walks on, over the crest, and out of view. When we arrive at the crest, he has gone. We don't see him on the lane that stretches toward the sea and flattens out as it passes through a grassy field.

We stop and look at each other then back to the scene. Okay, he's really shy. They look at each other, then at me. We shrug our shoulders in the same moment, look around for him again, then continue our trek.

They start talking about where to eat lunch. My stomach growls out loud, and they all grin. I smile and feel a quick flush on my face. After referring to their phones, they decide we have no choice but to press on to a town called Markina-Xemein. I had eaten the one snack I had for today hours ago. Eugenia has a bag of nuts and shares them around. I take a few.

Camino arrows take us to higher elevations. The scenery changes dramatically. We pass through forests of pine trees.

There are logging operations on nearby slopes, reminding me of the Olympic Peninsula.

Sofia, Eugenia, and Claudia walk ahead of me in a triangle like a phalanx protecting me from the future. I don't feel my grandmother's presence, her protection.

Our path comes to a large clear-cut. "Markina is down there, in the valley," says Eugenia as she points out the town far below.

The gravel road turns into a dirt trail beside a plantation of pines. The air feels clean, the sky hangs bright blue, and the smell of this pine forest tickles memories of Michael and me running and playing near the camp. These trees are twelve to fifteen inches in diameter at the base and perfectly spaced. From the piles of fresh-cut logs we have seen, I'd guess these live trees are nearly ready for harvest. On the single-track trail, we walk along like a gaggle of wandering geese. Returning to the shade of the trees makes for comfortable hiking, and we begin to lose altitude with each step.

Not paying attention, and in a daze of contentment, I almost run into the back of Claudia. She has stopped dead in the trail, and now steps to one side. Eugenia and Sofia have stepped off the trail as well. They stare at something on the ground.

Scratched into the soil and down the trail we see my name in neatly scribed letters.

My skin goes clammy. I look to my trail companions. Each face I see has a concerned look.

"Okay, yes, a little creepy," Sofia says sarcastically. A murmur of assent comes from the others.

"I don't know what to think," I say as I stand there looking at the letters in our path. I want to believe he's just not any more comfortable with people than I am. Right now, though, I'm confused.

They close in on me a little. A little too much. Sofia says it for them, "You need to watch out for him. I hope I'm wrong. Still, stay aware."

I nod in agreement, and we begin walking. How do I feel about Rond? He seems injured somehow. The look in his eyes when I saw him on the trail, sitting on a stone, it reminded me of my young friend. Michael seemed creepy at times, too, but he was completely harmless. What has become of my little friend?

The outskirts of Markina, nestled in a verdant valley, breaks from the forest. Eugenia, today's tour guide, leads us to an oddly shaped church beside the Camino. Inside are stones the size of trucks leaning against each other like a tripod. Beneath the monoliths stand an altar and a shrine with a statue. I stop before it, lean in, and read its placard. An idol of St Michael. I see my friend's face in the Saint's image. Gooseflesh crawls over my skin under the long-sleeved sun shirt I'm wearing.

I join the others. Traipsing in our goose-gaggle, we stroll around the stones, and then out into the joyous warmth of the sun.

I look back through the doors to the statue of St. Michael, wishing I could take him along with me today, to keep him safe at my side.

"Like, that was interesting," says Claudia, interrupting my thoughts.

"My stomach is grumbling," says Sofia.

We pass through pristine parks and enter a plaza in the center of town. A vibrant energy of voices and laughter fills the square. We glance from one sidewalk café to another, then select a table close by. The Germans order beer and I ask for water.

Sofia settles into her chair and fusses with her pack. "Where do you think our odd young man went?" She looks around for our thoughts on the subject. I hunch my shoulders and let them fall. I recall the sight of my name scratched onto the trail and how it made me feel, unsafe and more than just uncomfortable.

Father Ernesto telling me to stay vigilant for my safety comes to mind.

Our drinks come, and later our meals. Sitting with these women is something I have never done before. I'm uptight, but the conversation feels light. They thankfully speak in English for my benefit, and I am amazed by how well they speak it. Claudia was an exchange student in Alabama and later studied in Denver Colorado, so my ears have an easier time with her accent. The conversation is mostly about the Camino, who they have met along the way, and people they know who have been to Spain before. Sofia and her father had walked a portion of Camino from France, the Camino Francés, the most popular route, at age sixteen. I start to relax, settling back into my seat, a tall glass of water on my lap, wrapped by all ten digits. I could watch and listen to these women all this lovely day.

People come and go, stop to visit friends, sit for a glass of wine and conversation. Beside our table four women sip white wine and talk lively and cheerily about who knows what. They appear my grandmother's age. I look away, then over to Sofia. She is the cheery one in our group.

By the time we decide we should return to the trail, the others have settled on stopping at the monastery where my plan says I will stay the night. Reading about it on my Norte app, it seems like a hostel, we will sleep in common rooms. I have not done so without my grandmother. I can do this. I hope.

And what if Rond shows up? Is he a good person or not? I wish my grandmother could answer these questions for me.

Bolibar, Spain
August 6, 1982
Have been hiking in the mountains for a while now. We don't have those marvelous sea views. Not many people hike this route to Santiago, but I have made a couple of friends. Fred, an adventurous American and his "travel buddy," Gloria, walked the Camino Francés two years ago. They have told me about crossing the Pyrenees, of quaint villages, and the wide-open meseta.

From Georgia's Travel Journal

TWELVE

Zenarruza, October 9, 2019

The climb to Zenarruza is long, yet enchanting (using one of Lou's recent favorite words). A full and happy stomach after lunch, the warm afternoon air, the green valleys, and cute Bolibar town put me in a thoughtful mood. I think again about Georgia walking this very same route so many years before me, feel her pulling me along.

I have met some people now, made friends. They share far more with me than I do with them, and they want to help me with a strange Norwegian boy. I'm still not sure about him, but I think—though I think too much—he's harmless. What I see in Rond is pain, that he has been hurt somehow, in some deep-inside way.

Returning to the beauty around me and our final climb for

the day, I see my new friends not far ahead. I easily catch up to them.

In a line, the Germans and I enter the courtyard between a collection of old and new buildings in this large monastery complex. Other pilgrims wander about, sit on steps, or stretch out on the lawn. We make our way to the gift shop where we will register for the night. Claudia goes first, then me. After our credentials are stamped, a monk—who looks desperately like Father Ernesto—guides us to our dorm room. It's in a newer part of the facility, in a room with a kitchenette, a half-dozen bunks, and a long table in the middle of the room.

He explains the evening's schedule in the bored tone of someone who has said these very words a thousand times before. I understand. "Coffee or tea with your pie, today?" rings from my memories of time behind the counter at Grandma Pat's café.

What will become of her place? José and Katie run the café now, but long term? I don't know. I don't want to think about it, not now.

We make our choices from available bunks around the room. Sofia and Eugenia return to the gift shop for beer brewed by the monks. Claudia and I decide showers are of higher priority.

The trickle from the shower is barely warm, and the shower rooms chilly, yet perfect. Each day on the Camino, the hiking part of the day ends with me tired of the stinky clothes I'm wearing. Soon after, I am showered and clean. I rinse out the smelly things. Each day similar in this way.

Outside, I find an empty stretch of pipe banister edging the patio, a driveway below. I spread my clothes along the railing in the sun for my things to dry. Claudia sits on one of the few deck chairs and chats with a Spanish man and an older man who sounds like he comes from the US.

Finished with my chores, I turn to the sun, leaning back onto the rail, and close my eyes. I soak in the marvelous rays, basking like a happy lizard.

"You sleep here this night, yes?"

My eyes fly open. It's Rond, right there in front of me, stealing the sunlight. I almost fall backward and tumble over the railing to the asphalt below. Again, too close, my protective bubble invaded. He has a beer in his hand and the smell of it on his breath. I slide sideways down the rail, wiping my damp clothes into a crumpled heap. Claudia has stopped talking.

Rond follows me. "Sleep here, yes?"

Finally, I find words. "Yes, we do. Hello, Rond." I turn away and rearrange my things on the handrail. "We didn't see you this afternoon."

When I turn back, he is still there. This is the first time I have seen him without his backpack and big blue poncho. He is very thin and looks taller now. He stands over me, his shock of yellow-orange hair blazing with the sunlight behind him, his face shaded and difficult to see.

I hear their voices first: Sofia and Eugenia round the corner coming from the courtyard, beers in hand, an extra one for Claudia. They freeze at the tableau before them. The men with Claudia are not talking. The world has frozen.

Rond makes a half-turn toward Sofia and Eugenia. He drops his head to one side, a quizzical look on his face. "I am sorry," he says as he turns to me. "I go now." He walks away, his head hanging low.

The rest of us slowly thaw. Claudia and the others come to me.

"You okay?" asks Sofia.

"Yeah, sure. He startled me, that's all."

"He's an odd one, that boy," says Claudia with a forced southern drawl. We all smile.

Sofia hands a beer to Claudia who takes a long drink from the bottle, leans forward a little bit, and almost spits it out.

"Not German beer," says Eugenia. They chuckle. Claudia struggles to keep the brew from spewing out her nose.

Eugenia says, "There are many people on the lawn, playing and enjoying the last of the sunlight. We came to get you two. The beer gets better after the first one," she says as she nods at the one in Claudia's hand.

I have no objections, which surprises me. Crowds are not my thing. Claudia calls to the men she had been talking with and we all stroll back to the courtyard and the gift store.

Rond is there, sitting alone on a large stone at the edge of a large, thick lawn. A boy throws a stale baguette for a large dog who fetches it and chews on it until the boy calls her back. Here and there are groups of pilgrims and tourists chatting, some sitting cross-legged, some lying down, stretched out and taking it all in.

Claudia introduces Juan and Brian, and they resume their conversation from before. Once their beers are gone, Sofia and Eugenia leave to get cleaned up. Rond watches me.

Pushing as hard as ever against my natural hesitancy, I walk over to him and stand in the setting sun, shading him, looking down on him. "Yes, I do stay here tonight. We didn't see you today?"

"I . . . Please sit," he says.

Still uncomfortable and tense, I move to the side and settle on the lawn. He slides off the rock and sits across from me. I see he has a new beer. He notices this and reaches out, offering it to me.

"No thanks."

"Is good beer," he says. This makes me smile because of what the Germans think of the monk's home brew. He sees this reaction, looks intently into my eyes. I fear he has taken my smile the wrong way. My insides tighten even more.

He leans in. "Your eyes . . . they look glacially blue, icy." He has said the word in four syllables, sort of singsong, *glay-see-ah-lee*. "Glaciers, you have seen before, yes?"

People often refer to the color of my eyes but have never called them icy. "No. Not up close. On the Olympic Peninsula, where I lived with my parents, we could see some, but far away."

"In Norway, my home, we have many. You say *mucho* in the Spanish, yes?"

"Yes. Sí," I reply as I try on a thin smile.

He asks a few more questions about the Spanish language. Then he drains his beer and goes for another. Claudia and the men have followed the sun and sit closer to me now. I can overhear their conversation. I happily sit and soak in the sun, propped back on outstretched arms, face to the sky, eyes closed. The fragrances of freshly mowed grass, a flowery aroma like jasmine, and pine and eucalyptus trees tickle the membranes of my olfactory system.

Rond returns with two open beer bottles in hand. As he sits, he extends one to me. "A clean bottle for you."

"I don't drink," I say.

"Oh, is good beer. Try it," he says, while poking his arm straight toward my face.

"No, Rond. I don't like beer. And, besides, like I said, I don't drink."

"You must try. Is good beer." He keeps the beer extended to me, takes a drink from his bottle, and hums a note of pleasure.

"Try, is very good."

"No thanks," I say with a forceful tone as I scoot away from him.

"Is good beer, very good," Rond says while pushing the beer toward me.

"Let it go, dude," says Brian, the American man. He is

standing now, Claudia at his side. The world seems to freeze in place again, everything beyond us a blur.

"Again, I do it, Summer, yes?" says Rond as he lowers his face.

Before I can respond he gets up and walks away, his arms hanging low, the beer bottles dangling from his fingertips.

I am sitting up, legs crossed at the ankles, arms wrapped around my legs. My icy-blue eyes look at the ground and Claudia's feet.

"He tries too hard with you, Summer."

"I guess so." I want to think he's harmless, wounded but harmless.

Claudia sits on the grass beside me. "Are you okay?"

"Yeah. I don't know what to do. Should I leave, go home? Maybe I shouldn't be here."

"No, Summer. Please don't leave. We are with you. We can watch out for Rond," she says as she looks into my eyes.

I glance up and we both smile. "He. . . we don't know what he has been through."

"That is right," she says. "We haven't walked in his shoes, as you might say."

"My grandmother says things like that." I want to hug Claudia. My Grandma Pat too.

We sit quietly for a while longer. I start to hear the conversations around me again. The sun settles behind the trees and the air begins to cool. Time for my coat.

Something called *vespers* happens at seven-thirty. Afterward, dinner gets served in our dorm room. Many of the pilgrims want to attend tonight's services. Eugenia talks me into going along with them. I had planned to read more of my great-aunt's journal and would have happily stayed by myself for a while. But I find I am curious.

A few minutes before the appointed hour, people stream out

the door and head for the church. I join the Germans and we start for the door. Claudia reaches up, puts a hand on my shoulders, and says, "You should cover your shoulders and arms."

I stop, confused.

"To go into a church, you should cover up. And put some shoes on, too," Eugenia says as she looks at my bare feet, white tape wrapped around one toe and both of my heels. Being barefoot is a happy habit of mine. I have run around bare foot most of my life. "Anything you have. It's a sign of respect."

I flush so red I fear my hair color has changed. I return to my pack, pull out a puffy jacket and put it on while slipping angry feet into my trail shoes. Not daring to tie them, I tuck the laces into their respective shoe.

We venture out into the evening and join the others in the old church. I glance about for Rond.

Eugenia leans in. "Where is he?"

Our eyes search the large room. Not seeing him, we take our seats behind other pilgrims. They are young and old; thin and heavy. There's a pious woman, much older than my grandmother, thumbing through a Bible, intently studying the text. And there are the simply curious people, like me.

The monks file in and seat themselves on the dais. The musty smelling chamber falls silent. Behind us the door opens with a loud, grating creak. Everyone looks around at the disturbance. It's Rond. His head hangs low. The door squeaks closed. He slips into a pew behind us. The space within these stone walls quickly falls silent again.

Claudia, on the opposite side of me, leans in. I look around, inspecting the church this time. She says, "Vespers means evening prayer. They hold these services every evening. It's a canonical time for Roman Catholics."

I turn back to her.

"Once upon a time, I was a catholic," she says.

The service begins.

Everything is in Spanish or Latin and I have never been to church services before. I sit quietly, worried what the young man behind me may do, and take in as much of the scene as I can.

It's amusing watching these monks. They fuss with this or that and then speak their part when the time comes. They look very different from one another. And I'd say most of them drink a fair amount of their home brew.

One especially large guy has a difficult time staying awake. I try to imagine their lives here, doing this every day, feeding pilgrims for our donations, tending gardens and brew kettles.

I finish roaming through what I imagine of the monk's lives here. The evening's vespers end. We stand and file out of the church. Rond folds into the crowd not far behind me.

We, a meandering line of tired pilgrims, return to our dorm. As we file into the room, a large pot of thick, marvelous smelling soup filled with pasta noodles and a tray with loaves of freshly baked bread are delivered to our table.

As I sit down, I look around for Rond. He is not here.

The meal looks amazing. I have such a huge appetite, I could drain the large bowl all by myself.

Conversations spring up around the table. I cannot keep up. So many people in this tight space. And the roar of so many voices at once. One day I hope I'm better at this, more comfortable in such settings. In my grandmother's café I stayed behind the counter, used it as my shield. It's different here. My shield, now, is only my mind and where it will wander.

Today's trek was filled with emotional highs and lows, through such beautiful countryside and reflective moments, which lasted for hours; lunch with the Germans, watching them interact as normal people do; the uncomfortable moments when around Rond; and wondering if Grandma Pat's presence will return to me. Before coming to Spain, I never really experienced life, humanity. Not truly. I know this, now.

I know I want to meet more people like these German friends. Yes, I want to laugh with them and hear their stories. And I want to know our young Norwegian, know what has hurt him. I do want all this. But in this minute, I also want to get away. I need space to regroup, figure out how to do all those things. I want what the others have. All these people here tonight happily talk and laugh and share their stories. Can I, someday?

A monk returns for the pots and a detail of pilgrims starts washing the dishes and returning them to their shelves. I could help them. But the urge to run feels more powerful; I have failed. I bowl my way out the door and into the darkness. Stars dot the night sky. The cold night air hits me in the face, and it feels great.

The voices from inside die away. A handful of pilgrims also enjoying the night air eventually returns to the dorm room. The tightness in my muscles begins to release. A yawn the size of a lion's roar consumes me. I give the others a few minutes, take in the night air, and then follow them inside.

The room falls near to silence. A gentle snore ripples from an older man in one corner, a murmur of conversation in another. I slip into my bag and hit the pillow. The lights are turned off.

As the fuzz of sleep approaches and my tense, tired muscles continue to relax, only one nagging question rests on my mind: How will it go with Rond tomorrow?

Bilbao, Spain
August 8, 1982
We found a hostel in the city center that has a courtyard, a rare treat, I'm told. We all found rooms, my new friends and me. Now drinking beer and listening to them make plans for the next few days. Plans are overrated.

From Georgia's Travel Journal

THIRTEEN

Zenarruza, October 10, 2019

The monastery's bells ring out. I sit straight up, my sleeping bag hanging from my shoulders, twists of my hair snag in the springs of the bunk above me.

It's still very dark outside but I hear people stirring, the rustle of bags and gear, shoes scraping across the linoleum floor. I look at my phone, it's only six a.m. Monk's hours, not mine. I free myself, lay back down, pull my bag up, and curl into a ball. The bells continue their assault: deep-toned peals, followed by a series of high-pitched tolling.

More pilgrims get up to prepare for the day. Last night, I thought about today and Rond. Should I leave early today, go off on my own again, avoid him, spend time alone on the trail? I could spend more time with the Germans. Or find a way to understand the Norwegian.

I'll sleep a while longer. The last ring of the bells tapers away as slow as a receding flood. It does not get light for a while yet. I'll wake with the sun and decide then.

Before I can fall asleep again, the room is a chamber of racket. I cannot tell if there are three noisy people up getting ready to go or all of them. Except me. Then it hits me. I need to pee.

I slip out of my bag, find my hoodie and headlamp and head for the restrooms. My long, bare legs stick out from under my hoodie. The others can't see me because of the darkness, but I feel covert glances and pull the sweatshirt down, stretching the fabric.

As I return, and under a dim light over the patio area, I see a couple of men buckle their backpacks as they start to walk into the dark. Their headlamp beams spear the darkness as they start their day.

Inside, there are a few others getting ready to leave, red lights from headlamps illuminating their gear, flashing this way and that. Near as I can tell in the dark, most of the others are still in their bunks. I sit quietly on the edge of mine and again consider my options. The lights go on. I hear a guttural groan from one corner. I look toward the sound. At one end of a balled-up heap in a dark blue sleeping bag, I see a stack of yellow-orange curls. I look around and see Sofia, Eugenia, and Claudia, still sleeping in their bunks. Rond groans again and rolls over, face to the wall.

Decision made. I'll leave, quick as I can.

The monks had left bread and jams for our breakfasts. A tall, older man heats water in the microwave for instant coffee. Nearly ready to go, and with my backpack hanging from one shoulder, I spread jam on a hunk of bread and head for the door. It's still dark outside, but a hint of dawn slides up from the east. With the bread hanging from my mouth, I buckle my backpack, turn on my headlamp, and start the day's long walk.

I leave the monastery grounds and the Camino dives into a

thick forest then begins a gentle climb. The darkness and the aloneness send a shiver across my back. *This is what you wanted.*

Once it's light enough, I store my headlamp and refer to the plan on my phone. Today's route wanders over twenty-five miles. Sofia and her friends talked about a shorter day. They may stop in Gernika. I plan on Lezama. Tomorrow, I need to pass through the large city of Bilbao. I want to blast through there, not have to stay the night, so walking, and surely suffering, a long day today will make that possible.

The Camino is the familiar mix of trails and paved lanes, arrows, and splashes of yellow paint marking the way. Before leaving San Sebastián, I had read about how the Camino del Norte is always up or down, seldom flat. True, so far. They say the Camino Francés, inland from here, has hundreds of miles of flatlands to cross. Today is through more forested hills.

The Camino and the morning go by quickly. I pass through the tiny villages of Muntibar, Olabe, and Marmiz, and soon come to Gernika. As usual, my stomach raises a fuss. I'll stop for a bite to eat.

The café I select is small but bright inside—and quiet. I order something called a *bocadillo* and an orange juice from the woman behind the bar.

Outside of the tall plate-glass windows, a few pilgrims pass by on the street outside, none of them stopping. I again look at my route for the day and find the albergue I had planned for tonight. According to the Camino del Norte app, my next bunk waits for me twelve miles from here.

The woman sets the bocadillo, a huge sandwich, in front of me. It's nearly the size of a bread loaf and has a thick mixture of scrambled eggs in its middle. Oh. My. Goodness.

Before returning to the Camino, I finish most of the sandwich and store the rest in my pack. It's warmer still outdoors. My backpack needs a few adjustments before I can settle into an easy stride.

The only thing to disturb my peace is a hotspot stinging one of my heels. Now I think twenty-five miles was a bad idea. Too late.

My mind wanders about as I walk. I think of Georgia dying so young but first getting to see so much of the world. My thoughts roll across the Spanish countryside to a place where someone is mailing out the journal pages. And they settle on the idea that Georgia searched for her "wayward" father.

And I wonder things like, *where are the German women? Where is the guy from Norway?*

A pain in my heel disrupts my daydreaming. I stop to see what I can do to fix this new blister. Thankfully, the skin has not broken. I tape a piece of padding over it and return to the day's long walk.

After a few more hours of walking, I hope I'm close to the albergue and my next shower and a place to lie down. The sun hangs low, long shadows cover the trail, and the temperature falls. My stomach complains again. I round a corner and walk down a long, steep gravel road, my feet aching, the new blister now screaming. At the bottom of the hill, I see a sign for the *Albergue Guillermo*.

In front, I find a crumbling stone wall and a bent, rusted iron gate. As I come closer, I see a chain around the gate, locked up tight. *What the hell?*

A tattered and weathered sign hangs on the gate. I look beyond the metal bars to the building. It's not much to look at, but I want in there so bad it hurts. No, that's my feet and legs. The spot where Maria had bandaged my ugly blister throbs painfully. The heel of the opposite foot burns. My tired hands fight to release the buckles of my backpack. I slide the straps off my shoulders and let the now-familiar demon slip down my back, over my ass, and to the ground.

I yell out, "Anybody there?"

Nothing. It's so quiet I can't stand it. I pull the phone out of my pocket and look at the map. It's still miles before the city of Bilbao. I glance in both directions of the Camino, then look up. There's not much light left in the day. I could walk on with my headlamp. My feet protest. I want to crumble into a heap right here, and weep.

Looking at the sign on the gate, I see a phone number. *What the heck, give it a try.*

I try without success a couple of times before remembering I need to use the Spanish country code. This time it rings.

"Hola."

"Hello. Um, hola. Do you speak English?"

"A little, sí, señorita."

"I am at the albergue. Outside the gate. It's locked."

"Ah, sí. Está clo-sed."

"What?" What is he saying? "Dammit," I say and start to shed huge drops of salty tears. Where did they come from? I hope this man cannot hear me cry.

"Espere ahí," he says, and hangs up.

Crap. What did he say? I know this. What was it? Wait. He said to wait.

As this mini storm swirls inside my cranium, I hear a bang, then footsteps crunching on the gravel path. They come my way—from inside the gate.

"Señorita. Albergue está clo-sed," says the scruffy looking man on the other side of the iron bars. He is unshaven and has long, wild white hair, his clothes nearly worn threadbare. Tears sting my eyes again and stream hot down my face. All strength leaves my body. I grasp the iron gate to keep from melting to the ground. "Señorita," he says and begins unlocking the gate. "Ven, ven. Come. You rest."

My tears stop. But I need to sit. At least for a few minutes.

The scruffy fellow picks up my pack, leads me to the front door, and beckons me inside. I see paint buckets and tools strewn about. One corner of this first room we come to appears bright and clean with a new coat of paint, the rest of the room a shambles.

"You rest, sí?"

I nod in response, then take a seat on a stool near a long counter outside of a narrow kitchen area. I introduce myself with a voice so quiet I doubt he has heard me.

The man leans my backpack against a stool beside me and puts out a hand. "Teléfono?"

He is clever, knows how to use my phone to translate for us. His paint-speckled fingers type fast. He hands the device back to me, I read it, then do the same.

He tells me his name is Guillermo, but his friends call him Memo. He has been working all day, repainting the inside of his albergue. He plans to walk the short distance to his home very soon. He leaves me to rest and starts picking up his tools and closing pails of paint.

Once again, I consider walking into the night, walking into a huge city I know zilch about. God, I'm so tired. I translate and ask Memo if he knows of another place I could stay, anything, anywhere close by. He stops, looks up and tilts his head. I half expect him to rub his whiskered chin in this contemplative moment.

"No, señorita, nada."

I don't need a translator for this batch of bad news. I reach for my backpack and pull out the headlamp.

Memo has finished collecting what he needs and comes to me. He looks at the headlamp in my hand. "No, no. You no go.

Está tarde." He asks again for my phone, and we resume the type, read, type, read routine.

It takes much longer for his meaning to sink in than the translation does. He says I can stay at his place, sleep on his couch.

I look to him. He says, "Sí," as he nods his head. "Está bien, is okay." He picks up my backpack and holds it out for me to put on. "I cook bien, también." Again, no smartphone required.

Grandma Pat would freak.

Memo locks the gate behind us, and he leads as we walk down the road. Within a few minutes we come to a well-kept block house, set back from the road. He beckons me to follow. It's nearly dark by now. And I'm the one about to freak. A rush of cold air flows down from the nearby trees and settles on me. I begin to tremble.

I know the look in my father's eyes when he wants to help. And I remember the gleam in Paul's eyes when he wanted me. I tell myself I know the difference.

Memo opens the door, flips a light switch, and stands aside to let me into his home. I lean forward to look inside. My feet are frozen in place. Memo says, "Está bien." The chill on my skin sinks deeper. I look into his eyes, one last read of this man before I commit—or run. I have been running all day. I'm so damn tired. I glance inside the home again.

I turn to him once more. I see a kindness and concern in his dark eyes. My eyes linger on his face. He smiles a warm smile, then says, "You choose. Others, they stay. Some nights. Sí."

Yes, I need to decide. He does have kind eyes.

He steps through the doorway and leaves the door open for me.

I step inside the first room. Eyeing ancient furniture, I see the old sofa along one wall, a distinct sag in its middle. He indicates where I can put my things, then shows me to the kitchen, and then the bathroom. It, too, is tidy but worn. Memo wraps his arms around himself and scrubs at himself, telling me I can shower here. It's then I realize I'm taller than he is. Why now, I have no idea. But in his eyes, I do not see a bad man.

Still, in the bathroom I prop my backpack in front of the door while showering—for all the good it might do against a madman.

Clean and warm, I return to the kitchen. Memo slowly stirs a large pot on a gas stove. I'm not sure of the aromas, the spices he has used, but it smells delicious. A loaf of bread sits on a table, a serrated knife at its side. A feeling of comfort surrounds me, cuddles me. I can't quite imagine that this man wants to fatten me up to slaughter before sunrise.

Nor can I believe I am doing this, staying here.

After consuming the contents of my first bowl without regard for how great it tastes, I ask Memo what it is. "Fabada," he says. It's a soup of fabada beans and hunks of different meats. And, oh my, it tastes amazing? He fills my bowl again and points to the bread. I cut more slices from the loaf and savor every bite.

We converse some more, sliding the phone back and forth across the table when needed. Memo pours red wine for himself and a splash for me. I protest politely, but he tilts his head and with a happy frown, nods. I take the glass by its thick stem and sip as little as possible. An unfamiliar sensation bites at my tongue. Before now, I had no idea what wine tasted like.

After we eat, I help with the dishes, wash out the pot, and clean the stovetop. With our chores done, Memo shows me to the sofa. He stops there, points at my stuff and the sofa, and then cups his hands beside his head and tips it sideways. Oh, God, yes. I could sleep a week. Or can I? Memo leaves me and walks down the hallway toward his room.

I get out my sleeping bag.

Soon, I hear music playing a scratchy tune on a radio coming from down the hall.

Memo has left on an end table lamp. I look around the room. Do I hunt for demons or peepholes? I can't believe this, what I am doing. I leave my clothes on, slip into my bag, turn out the light, and lie down.

Tired as I am, I still don't think I will sleep a wink.

Laredo, Spain
August 11, 1982
As I write this, I can't believe I still want to find our father. Patricia, now home, was the one interested in him after Mom spilled the beans about him leaving us to go to Europe. Now, I'm the daughter searching for him. But at my own pace, by God.

From Georgia's Travel Journal

FOURTEEN

Lezama, October 11, 2019

Memo gets up at daybreak. He prepares for the day and makes breakfast. It's simple and delightful. Bread from last night, toasted to crunchy perfection, and a tangy olive oil to drizzle over it. He even found an old tea bag, stale but heartwarming. He is quiet. His long gray hair is a mess of tangles and his slippered feet grate across the tile floor, like sandpaper.

I've recovered from yesterday's effort and the surprising invite to stay in the home of someone I had just met. A man someone. I have also retaped my big toe, preparing for another day of trekking across Spain.

Who does that sort of thing? Aunt Tilly's words wiggle their way through my brain. A pang of regret blooms, deflating just as quick.

Memo and I say our goodbyes at the end of the path to his

house. He returns to work on his albergue, and I turn west toward Bilbao.

The huge city sits as an obstacle I want to put behind me. I have read it's a beautiful place, with a cathedral, lots of churches, many great restaurants, an amazing waterfront, and a stunning Guggenheim Museum. But it's not for me. *Wikipedia* says there are over one million people in the metropolitan area.

At the eastern edge of the city, I come to a fork in the Camino. A decision to make, an easy one. I take the high road. Above Bilbao city center, then an industrial area and the vast port, my path wanders through suburbs and forested parklands. This bit of civilization is a sight to behold—at a distance. It takes hours to complete the eighteen miles to Portugalete, where the Camino will turn inland again.

Lunch, earlier in the day, at a neighborhood café above Bilbao was short and sweet. As I enter Portugalete, my stomach starts at it again. There are many places I can stay the night. I don't feel the need to worry about sleeping on a sagging sofa. There's a pilgrim's hostel, many pensiones, and several hotels.

Along the waterfront, there are tourist shops and restaurants. I turn away from the port and climb narrow streets to find a peaceful place. After a few blocks and up ahead I see a bar at a street corner. It looks perfect. Inside, the usual affair—a long bar on one side, tables and chairs under street-side windows opposite. I survey a mixture of smells in the air: coffee, garlic, seafood. . . and . . . I think it's ammonia. A tall, handsome, older man and a short woman I assume is his wife, her hair tucked behind her ears, tinker at cleaning and straightening up behind the bar. As I settle my backpack against the wall, he comes out to my chosen table and hands me a plastic-coated card with *Carta* written across the top, a menu. I cast a smile to him, meant to convey my stomach's desires, and order a hamburger.

Now, my stomach satisfied, and a quick review of tomorrow's

trek done, I realize it's getting dark outside. A corkboard with businesses pinned up in complete disarray droops from wires at the end of the bar. As I glance from one card or scrap of paper to another looking for a pensión I may have read about in my Norte app, the bartender comes to my side. I glance at him.

"Un pensión?"

"Yes. Sorry. Sí, señor," I say.

He points to one of the cards and says, "Nuestros amigos, allí. Good people."

As I pay for my meal and gather my things, the bartender draws me a quick map with directions to his friend's pensión, only a few blocks away. He also indicates where the Camino is, nearby, for in the morning. I collect my pack and wave to his wife before leaving.

I easily find the pensión. It is clean and quiet, has hot water, everything I need. After my shower, I settle into bed to reread from Aunt Georgia's journal.

Late the next morning, later than I'd have wished, gray light peeps through simple curtains, waking me from a deep sleep.

Breakfast, a fresh, buttery croissant and black tea, helps me wake up. I have hardly seen the owner of this establishment—only as I checked in last evening and as he mechanically dropped breakfast at my table overlooking the port.

The day's first meal complete, I gather my things and leave. The sun is high, peeking through thin layers of fog. As expected, I see Camino arrows at the first street corner I come to. Two people with backpacks are ahead of me as I climb the last few blocks and exit the city.

The route merges onto a pedestrian and cycling path beside a freeway, an easy stroll. Good thing because I, again, have more than twenty miles planned for today's trek.

By noon, I have returned to the sea. The town of La Arena, no more than a surfer's hangout, is more modern than what I have seen before. A beach stretches west of town. Many surfers wait, then catch their perfect wave under the foggy sky. Today is cooler, the hiking easy and pleasant. I walk alone most of the time. Pilgrims swap greetings as they pass by, or I pass them. There is no one look or style of the peregrino. Some are old, many of them young; others fast, with light packs, or slow, with giant ones; even talkative, like Sofia from a few days ago, or aloof like me.

Aromas of fried seafood and the nutty, oh-my-goodness scent of coffee pull at me. I should keep going. I lose this little battle. Surprising myself, I order a café con leche, and a slice of egg and potato Spanish tortilla. Sitting at a table outside the restaurant, overlooking the gray sands and the foaming strip of green water, I watch other pilgrims passing by. Like me, some succumb to the allure of the restaurant and stop in for a bite. Surfers, too, pass by heading out to or returning from the sea. I have never surfed the waves. I could one day, I hope. These people, too, are varied, some young and beautiful, richly tanned. They look like they have come from everywhere in the world.

Finished with my meal, a bitter aftertaste of coffee on my tongue, I return to my trek. It is getting late. I'm not paying much attention to anything other than sorting my backpack and watching the surf and surfers. A yellow arrow points me to a boardwalk crossing a broad field of short sand dunes and tufts of seagrass. I tug at the shoulder strap to lift the backpack high and tighten the waist belt.

"Summer?"

I flinch and turn sort of sideways, still walking.

"Sofia," I say. She and Eugenia are behind me a few steps. I look past them. "Where's Claudia?"

"She met an American man," says Sofia with no follow through. Like this is all that needs said on the subject. I suppose it is. "We have not seen you in a while. Where is Rond, have you seen him?"

"No, not since the monastery. How about you two?"

"We saw him yesterday, outside of Bilbao," says Sofia. "He did ask about you. I think he's all right, just not sure of himself or how to talk to people."

"I hope you're right," I say.

"He does like you, though," says Sofia, a tender smile on her face as she glances in my direction.

We continue walking, and I think about her statement. Is he likable?

At the other end of the beach, the Camino scales a rough, muddy stretch to a grassy plain above the sea. The sun burns through the fog and the views widen like a panoramic photo. The calm morning air floats a mingling of the scents of cattle, mown hay, and salty sea foam. The trail narrows, becomes deeply rutted at times; it takes more concentration then earlier today.

I'm still in the front of our trio. Rounding a tight, uphill bend I look up. It's like déjà vu. Rond sits on a rock ahead of us, waiting.

"Summer, hello. Hola, sí?" he stutters.

"Hola, Rond," I say. We have attracted the very guy with our curiosity.

"Hey, Rond," say the two other women in unison.

"I walk with you?" he says.

Sofia and Eugenia and I look to each other. I realize I'm the one to answer his question. "Yes, of course. How have you been?" Again, he has on the big blue poncho. He gets up and follows me. The others are close behind.

The paths we choose remain close to clifftops and occasionally drop to perfect little beaches. Each time, these stretches of sand remind me of a scene from my past. To steal away from my parents and their friends, I would hide out at a creek far from camp. There was a patch of sand and a sparkling swimming hole that would only see sunlight during the peak of summertime. Even Michael did not follow me there. I never took the same route to my peaceful place. Laura only came there the day Grandma Pat came to move me home with her. I miss her.

We trek along together, us chatting, Rond silent. Along the path are a few familiar faces. An older French couple from the night at the monastery, an Italian couple I have seen a few times. They seem very nice but have a hard time communicating with us. We did learn they are from Como, beside a lake of the same name. During my past life, I knew Bob from Wyoming and Gert from Minnesota. Now, in a week or two, I have met people from around the globe.

Rond, not far ahead of us, stops and looks back to me. As I approach, he says, "I am hungry. I eat there." He points to a grassy, rounded mound overlooking a miniature beach bordered with rocks, the surf lifting from them in clouds of spray. "You stop, too?"

I'm caught; what should I say? I look to Sofia, the more confident of our trio. She'll see *help* written on my face.

"There's a town not far ahead. Eugenia and I had talked about stopping there for lunch," says Sofia. Eugenia looks at her friend with a questioning eye.

"Sounds like a good idea," I say and look at Rond. This is not what he had hoped for, but he tags along with us after our wordless decision.

We find a quaint café in the next village. Sofia and Eugenia order beers. Rond decides not to join them. He and I order fresh-squeezed orange juice instead. One at a time we select pre-made sandwiches from under a glass-covered tray ("pilgrim sandwiches," Eugenia calls them) on the bar and return to our seats. We remain quiet as we eat. Rond devours his meal and gulps down the juice, then sits there with arms crossed—mostly looking in my direction. I want to ask him about his writing my name on the trail. I want to know more about him. But I say nothing, ask nothing. The Germans survey Rond and me over their beers as they sip from chilled glasses.

After the town and lunch and filling our water bottles, we stroll along in the sun. Sofia, Eugenia, and I happy in our own little worlds. Rond stays quiet.

It's a spectacular day. I recall one paragraph I read from my great-aunt's journal last night:

"The sky along the north coast of Spain is a brilliant, bluebird blue, and as the fog burns off come late morning, the sea only a shade or two darker."

We walk on, Rond still quiet. Me not much better. He stays close to me. Walking across a long beach, I can hear Sofia and Eugenia chatting behind us. They come to some special topic, laugh out loud, and then chatter some more. Rond comes closer still, and rubbing shoulders with me while we walk, he says, "On we go. Yes?"

I pull away and look at him. He has an odd look in his eyes. My body tenses and I slow down. Sofia and Eugenia quickly catch up to us. They have seen our interaction, my involuntary response.

Rond huffs and walks off at a fast pace.

"You okay, Summer?" asks Sofia.

"Yeah, sure," I say.

"You need to kick him where it hurts," says Eugenia.

"No," I say. "I could never."

"You need to tell him how he makes you feel when he does those things," Sofia says as she moves in beside me. "I don't know if he realizes."

I look from side to side, Eugenia to Sofia. Kicking someone—however creepy they seem—is not my way. But then, neither is talking about my feelings.

They allow me to make up my mind, and we walk on.

By the time we come to another beach we can't see Rond. The tide lies farther out now, and we find a rock to sit on for a break. They don't mention him. Neither do I. But I feel the topic there. We know we will see him again, which rests on my shoulders heavier than my backpack. They plan to stay at the muni in Castro-Urdiales. I prefer being on my own, yet I also like being with these two women. And what of Rond?

I could go on by myself, want to go on by myself. I can manage; I've been successful so far. And I miss my grandmother, the warmth I feel when her presence joins my day. It's like the glow of a fireplace from across a room. A chill runs up my spine. We—Grandma Pat and I—should go on. Several hours of light remain in this day.

We stroll into and through Castro-Urdiales and find the municipal albergue at the far edge of town. It sits back from the main street, up on a short hill. Pilgrims and surfers crowd the front lawn and a line of people waiting to check in trails out the door. Sofia and Eugenia walk up the narrow sidewalk and slip into line. They take off their packs. I have stalled at the street.

My two companions turn and see my hesitation. "Will you stay here or go back into town?" asks Eugenia. I stand frozen, incapable of making a decision. A couple of skinny girls in bikinis come flying out of the repurposed house, hastily pushing through people in the doorway. One chases the other and they squeal. Loud as screaming monkeys.

"I think I'll walk on to Islares. It's not far." The next place to find a bed sits six miles away, but I cannot stay here. Sadness pulls at their faces, but they nod, both understanding my need.

Santander, Spain
August 18, 1982
Working at a café in the city center for a few days I earned money enough to call Mom, for all the good it did. She was fine, Patricia and Tilly were fine. She wouldn't tell me more about Father. So, I called our neighbor Maddy. They were good friends too. She said I walked the wrong route to find clues about him. I will return to Pamplona, take to the Camino Francés.

From Georgia's Travel Journal

FIFTEEN

Laredo, October 13, 2019

The Camino has again changed from muddy path to paved lane.

From bushy, green clifftops I now see the beachside town of Laredo. I will stay there tonight, following a short twelve-mile day. Yesterday's hike went long to avoid the crowded albergue in Castro-Urdiales. Today I've spent mostly in contemplation, looking backward. Back to the beginning of my family's Camino and the mystery of the journal pages. And I've missed my new friends. I'm still curious about Rond, and what I will say to him when we meet again. And much of the day I've been reflecting on why I don't like people.

My conclusion, if I were to write one down—it's not that I dislike people. In the last two weeks I have met many fun, happy, smart, helpful souls I now call friends. Where I grew up, people, my parent's friends, were different. They could hardly take care of themselves, and they were seldom nice. But better people fill this world. I will write this into the pages of a journal—if I ever start one.

I check in for the night at the first albergue I come to, a private one. First order of business, a peaceful hot shower. Then wash out a few things. Now my sleeping bag and most of my clothes dangle from a clothesline in a broad patio behind the building.

Between short naps I again read from Georgia's journal. I have retraced the parts to where I am now, to Santander farther along the coast, and then to her decision to change to the Camino Francés. The details are few, but she had heard from her mother's friend, Maddy, that her father, my great-grandfather, had followed information to a job in Pamplona. When the work was finished there, he started walking the Francés toward Santiago, taking odd jobs where he could.

I can no longer keep my eyes open. Why did he write to Maddy? Was it guilt? Was it also a tether to home?

The old journal now lays across my belly. If not for hunger, sleep would consume me. I can hear voices, more pilgrims stopping in for the night. The albergue only has a dozen bunks, all along one wall of this dark room. I chose a bottom bunk. From here I cannot see my things on the line outside. I'm not worried about them; I have the important bits with me: phone, passport, money, my grandmother's wallet, and the journal pages containing a part of my family history.

A growing din of voices intrudes from the sitting room beyond the doorway to my left. No more quiet time for me, I gather my things, throw my legs over the side of the bed, and sit up. High enough now, I can see outside to the patio. I consider gathering my stuff and hear a group coming this way. I look toward the door.

"Summer!" It's Sofia, as bright and cheery as ever.

On her heels stride Eugenia, Claudia, the American man, Brian, from our night at the monastery, and another woman.

"Hey," I say as I set the journal aside and stand up.

They all dart for the bunks, except Brian. He stands aside and lets the women vie for the closest remaining lower beds.

From the bunk next to mine, Eugenia says, "How have you been? We have not seen you in a while."

"I'm good."

Sofia has the next bed over. "We will get cleaned up and go out to find something to eat. Are you hungry?" she says, a wide smile blooming on her face.

"Funny," I mouth to her.

Eugenia leans closer and says, "You've become too thin, my friend."

Sofia overhears this and adds, "You should drink German beer." A chuckle comes from Claudia, then they all stop.

"Have you seen him?" asks Eugenia.

"No. Not since the four of us walked together, what, two days ago?"

"The days do become a blur, don't they?" says Sofia as she sets her things out on the bed.

My things have dried, I have repacked what I don't need now, and my sleeping bag is laid out, claiming the bunkbed while we're out to dinner. The others have showered and are ready to go out. My stomach gurgles, fortunately, not too loud.

The woman who came off the trail with the others stands beside Sofia. She has a beaming smile. Sofia introduces us. "Cheng hails from Shanghai, China," she says. She is tall, striking, and speaks excellent English.

Not far away, we find a restaurant with a pilgrim's menu. These are rare treats because the restaurant will serve us a meal before eight o'clock, the normal opening time for Spanish eateries.

There are two items to choose from as a first plate, two for the second, and canned peaches for dessert. Oh, and, they have a German beer on their short list. I order sparkling water and sit back to take it all in. Conversations run all over the place, all over the world. The American man tells of trips to Asia and Africa. Sofia asks lots of questions, apparently interested in traveling to those continents one day. Cheng and Eugenia get to know each other. Cheng has been studying French in the city of Tours. Eventually, the subject of tomorrow comes up.

"Summer?" says Sofia. "We have heard about this famous albergue, this side of the city of Santander. People call it a "Don't miss" place on the Camino del Norte. They call it what, Claudia?"

"It's in Güemes," says Claudia. "They call it the Grandfather's Cabana, or some such, operated by a former priest who was born in the original house on the property."

Eugenia looks it up and says the official name.

"I remember reading about it," I tell them. "I plan to stay there."

"We should all stay there," says Sofia, who gets a happy nod of agreement from Cheng.

At daybreak, we quietly slip out of the albergue, walk through parts of Laredo, beside a long arc of beach to a ferry crossing a wide river to another town. After a bite to eat, we settle into a comfortable pace. "Walking speed," Claudia calls it.

The sky has been overcast, perfect for a long walk. Most of the way has been on blacktop roads and backroads. We are still together, the six of us. My feet are sore, a couple new hotspots forming. Ahead and up a steep driveway, Cabaña del Abuelo Peuto waits for us.

In a line, we file through a simple iron gate into the front yard and are immediately greeted by volunteers who offer food, water, and wine. Other groups are seated farther down a long picnic table. We set our packs aside and happily take a seat on the wooden benches. I untie and painfully slip off my trail shoes.

Piles of pasta salad, bread, and red wine are put in front of us. Another volunteer, an English woman, comes and sits with us to enter our details into a ledger and assign a dorm room and beds for the night to each of us. There are several buildings and a hundred beds at this albergue, the woman says. She goes through the evening's schedule. First, a greeting by Padre Ernesto, the man who owns and runs this place, in a room upstairs, then dinner, followed by religious services for those who wish to attend. The woman also talks about the many volunteers it takes to feed everyone and care for the place, but says she will leave the history of the albergue to Ernesto.

More pilgrims crowd in. I become overwhelmed by it all, by the number of people, and the frenetic energy so quick after a nice day on the Camino. I pull in deep breaths, and I hear *Suck it up, girl.* It's more of a feeling than something I hear with my ears, but boy is it familiar.

We are in the newest building, farthest from the main house. Each of us finishes our daily chores of showering, washing out clothes, and tending to feet. Dozens of people mill about, and newcomers are shown to their assigned beds. We hear some of the same information we had heard before and greet them with a nod and a cheerful "Hola."

Still desperate for space, I push aside a nagging feeling I should stay. I leave our dorm and stroll around the compound in bare feet, bits of white tape doing their best to remain in place. Out front, overlooking the valley we had crossed a couple of hours ago, tension unwinds from tired muscles. I calmly place one hand into the palm of the other behind my back, lean back, and with eyes closed, I sniff at the air. There's fresh-cut grass mixed with a hint of something sizzling in a pan. I let out a sigh and can almost feel the myofascial tissues in my quad muscles slipping, sliding into realignment after a hard day's work. This is a peaceful spot. I open my eyes. A few people sit around, chatting, or taking in the view and relaxing like me. I see why they built the original house in this very location.

Almost completely zoned out, I hear a loud clank. I ease my gaze toward the sound.

A big blue poncho slips through the now open gate and into the front yard. The marshmallow rotates and the gate closes with a click. The bright curls on top of his head spring about with his movements. Then he looks right to me, the first person he sees. Tension returns in a flurry, my breath catches, I try to fade back, but have nowhere to hide. I smile and nod.

He nods, looks away, and heads toward the table. A volunteer greets him with a smile, clipboard in hand. I watch the now-familiar proceedings for a while, then return to our dorm. Though I dread the idea, I should put on shoes for the meeting upstairs and for dinner.

Dozens of pilgrims have lined the walls of a circular room above a set of older dorm and shower rooms. Many more sit on pillows and mats cast about the center of the large room. The last rays of daylight give way and the room's lights are turned on. Rond sits directly across the wide circle from me.

A man, Padre Ernesto (yes, another Father Ernesto), enters the room at an angle from where I am. He snaps a few pictures with an expensive looking SLR camera. He's old, like really old, but still quite agile. He crosses the room and takes up a position close to a large map of this area of northern Spain. The padre stands tall and—in both Spanish and English—talks of being born here, being in the priesthood for a time, then traveling around the world, before returning and opening this place for pilgrims. He has done so many fantastic things in his life I marvel at it all. Tiring, Ernesto turns the meeting over to another man, who, through an interpreter he has chosen from the crowd, goes into the work they do and the work the money raised by our generous donations does around the world.

I listen as best I can to everything these men say, but Rond's presence and glances distract me. I remember my promise to myself. I can only hope he understands what I have to say, assuming I can get the words out.

After the meeting, we are invited to the dining room for the evening meal. I try to catch up to Rond but the crowd is too big, the passageways too narrow. I lose him, even with his bright shock of hair.

When we come to the dinner area I hear the crowd, the yammering of a million words at once. I draw in a breath and enter. I sit with my group of new friends at a table along the back wall. The noise becomes deafening as the room fills and volunteers haul huge bowls and platters of food and bottles of wine and water to the long tables. The space is comfy, with a huge stone fireplace, white walls, and natural wood accents. There are additional rooms with more tables to the right of us and to the left, near the kitchen. The ceiling hangs low. Cheng, taller than I am, ducks to move through the room to take a seat at our table.

I want to look for Rond but wondrous bowls of salad and penne pasta with vivid red and thick marinara sauce now have my attention. The aromas of fresh bread and herbs and wine and clean bodies fills the air. We load plates and pass bowls. Everyone talks at once—everyone. I very much want to take a plate of food back to our dorm, to have some space around me. When a wine bottle comes her way, Eugenia pours some into my glass, leans into me and says, "It helps. But you might go easy."

I do go easy, and it soon becomes apparent the wine does no good. I focus on satisfying my stomach, which keeps my mind off the walls and the bodies closing in on me. It also helps to focus on one conversation at a time. Eugenia sits on my right, Sofia on my left. We three talk mostly with each other, sometimes accepting and passing on a bowl of this or a bottle of that.

"We will walk through Santander tomorrow," says Sofia. "What are your plans, Summer?"

I have been dreading this moment. I like being on the Camino with these people, they are my Camino family. But the journal, Georgia's path, guides me elsewhere. "When I get to Santander, I will catch a bus to Pamplona."

They look to one another, and then at me.

"Have you decided to go home, to return to California?" asks Sofia.

Eugenia puts a hand on mine, a sincere look of concern on her face.

"No, no. It's not like that. I . . . there's this journal, you see, my great-aunt's travel diary. I have been following in her footsteps. At Santander she took a bus to Pamplona and continued her trek on the Camino Francés."

Eugenia lets my hand go and says, "When was this? When did your aunt walk the Camino?"

"In 1982," I say.

Their mouths drop open at the same time.

"Really?" asks Sofia, an odd tone to her voice. I can't tell if she is interested or disbelieving.

"Yeah. It's a long story. She—my Aunt Georgia—was following her father, my great-grandfather, who had come to Spain to escape the pain of his time at war in Asia."

Sofia and Eugenia stare at me. Interested, I decide.

Before they can ask the million questions behind their eyes, dinner has come to an end and Padre Ernesto stands to speak again. He summarizes the things said upstairs, the work they do around the world, and he points out the donations box on the wall by the door leading out to the front of the albergue—the door I've wanted to sprint through for the last hour.

Volunteers pick up empty bowls and plates and pilgrims file out the door. They stuff bills and coins into the donations box as they go. As do the three of us. On the patio I see Rond sitting alone, gazing out over the valley and the lights of farmhouses speckling the scene. His colorful hair blazes under a pearly hue from glimmering patio lights.

"I'm going to talk with him," I say to Sofia and Eugenia. They still bracket me like protective parents. Like Laura had done during my last few weeks at the camp.

"We'll stay with you," says Eugenia.

"No, that's okay. I see plenty of people around. It's all right."

They reluctantly leave, and I make my way across the patio.

Rond is perched on a rock wall again, his back to me. Tables and comfy chairs fill the patio, but he sits on stone. He is so odd. He hears the crunch of my steps in the coarse gravel and turns toward me. I sit on the wall at an arm's length from him.

"Hola," he says.

"Hello, Rond. How have you been? We haven't seen you in a few days."

He stretches out his legs and crosses them at the knees, clasps his hands together, letting them settle onto his thighs, and then twists to face me. His face, half shadowed and half lit by the dim lights, looks ethereal.

"I find you, yes?" he says. I catch the smell of red wine on his breath as it floats to me.

"Yes, I suppose you did." How much has he had to drink tonight? "Did you like the meal? I am simply stuffed."

He twists his face in a quizzical glance. "Stuffed?"

"Oh, yeah. I ate too much. I was so hungry, and it was so good I couldn't stop myself. So was the wine, yes?"

His gaze returns to the dark valley. "I see. I did not care for the wine," he says.

We sit quietly for a moment, simply looking at twinkling lights along the valley floor and up to the zillion stars above.

"Rond?"

"Yes."

"I grew up in a shack in the woods. The people, my parents and their friends, were drunks and druggies. I didn't fit in there. There was a man, my father's friend, who ran the camp. He . . . he liked women, pursued them. I mean he liked them a lot. Came to them often. As I got older, he started to like me too. Do you understand what I mean?"

"He came to you?"

"Yes, well, he tried to." I turn to look at Rond, wanting to see if he gets it. "That's when I went to live with my grandmother in California."

He looks to me, his expression flat.

My fingernails dig into my palms. "I guess what I am saying is, I don't find it easy to trust people, especially men who get too close."

Even in the low light, I can see Rond's face go ashen. He turns away and lowers his face. He stays quiet for a long time, then says, "I think I know you meaning. Your meaning. I understand what I do to you . . . and so wrong. I am sorry. Very sorry. I do not trust . . . do not trust anyone. Except you."

We don't talk for a few minutes, gazing again at the twinkling lights before us, the Milky Way fanning overhead.

"Can you tell me about you, about your home in Norway?" My heart still races, palms sweaty. *Get on with it, girl.* I can do this.

He turns back to me. There are deep frown lines draped down each side of his mouth and knifing into his chin. "My mother's name is Rondella. A Nigerian name. I never know my father, or who he be." Rond squirms in his masonry seat, crosses his arms, then nervously drops them, and continues. "She, my momma, she escaped Africa to Norway. But bad men took her, made her do things. She had me. We escaped them and moved to a new city, to Oslo. We live there now. She works . . . in restaurant she does. She sends me to school, to university one day, she says."

I sit quietly, unable to speak. We have shared personal parts of our lives with each other. I cannot imagine his mother's life, the things she has had to do to survive. How could I? And how can I think badly of her son.

"What brought you to the Camino de Santiago?" I ask, not knowing what else to say.

"My momma, she studies, at her church, sometimes makes me go. But she learns and tell me about the path, the Way." He looks at his hands now. He opens them, palms facing up, like he is reading them. "Walk the Camino for her, Momma said. I will continue my studies when I return to Oslo."

Pieces of our puzzle fall into place in my mind's eye. We look into each other's eyes. "We are friends now, Rond," I say. I feel a clarity I have not felt before.

"Now we are friends," says Rond. "We can walk together tomorrow, sí?"

"Yes." Now for the bad news. "But I will only go as far as Santander with you. You and the others."

"Santander?"

"Yes. I will go from there to Pamplona." I'm too tired to explain further, and hope he can wait for the whole story, wait until tomorrow.

"Pamplona," he says.

I stand up and look around. Everyone has gone inside, to bed. "Let's talk about it in the morning, over breakfast. I'm so very tired right now."

Santander, Spain
August 19, 1982
Leaving the city and as the bus passes by Santander Bay, I recall how sick Patricia got on the ferry from here to England last month. Poor thing; wretched, really. I still miss her.

From Georgia's Travel Journal

SIXTEEN

Güemes, October 14, 2019

As I walk from our dorm to the dining room, the air chills my skin. Tendrils of fog lie on the valley floor like feathery, milk-filled veins and capillaries.

I join the Germans and Cheng for breakfast. There are a dozen other pilgrims huddled in knots about the large room. They sip coffee or tea, quietly chatting. I dunk a teabag and watch vapors float above our table from the large mug, my mood calm compared to last evening.

Rond enters through the front door. I wave him over. I ask him to sit with us. The shocked looks on Sofia's and Eugenia's faces are comical. He takes a seat beside me, but not too close, I notice.

Stacks of pancakes and piles of fruit fill the center of our table. The conversation is light, Rond clumsily joining in a few times. Other people file in and head for the coffee urn. Some have eaten and prepare to leave.

"So, our last day together, huh, Summer?" says Eugenia. She's not looking to me but at Rond when she says this. Not fazed by this, he now concentrates on the correct amount of milk in his cup of coffee, stirring the mixture to a perfect latte brown.

"Yes, I'm sorry," I say as I remove the tea bag from my cup.

Rond, finally happy with his coffee, rotates to look at me. "You say last night we talk about this now, yes?"

"Of course, Rond. Thank you for understanding. I was so very tired by then." He beams at this. The women grin.

"I have explained to them," I wave in the direction of the German contingent of my Camino family, "I'm following a travel journal written by my great-aunt Georgia, who walked the Camino in the early 1980s."

Cheng's head snaps my way, and she says, "Hiyah," and throws her hands up in amazement.

We all have a good laugh. But Rond's face returns to the information he tries to understand.

"She followed her father, my great-grandfather, who had come to Spain before her."

"And you now follow her, this many years late?" says Rond.

"Yes," I say. "She, Georgia, heard her father may have found a job in Pamplona and then from there walked the Camino Francés, the route starting in France."

"Then is third . . . what you call . . . third generation, yes?"

"Yes, of course," I say, though I had never thought of my story in this way. "That's me, the third generation to walk the Camino." The thought tingles in my chest and a shudder works its way out of my body, coming from somewhere deep, and going out in every direction. Out to who knows where.

Bellies satisfied, we gather our backpacks and leave this

wonderful place behind, taking our memories with us out into a new day.

We've walked for a couple of hours now. Before us stretches a miles-long beach, wide at low tide. Santander can be seen far off in the distance, across a bay. The day is gray and windy. Rond's poncho flaps relentlessly. We have talked some but walk along mostly quiet. Cheng walks well ahead of us and happily chats with another pilgrim, a woman with a dark brown ponytail sticking out of her cap.

From the Norte app, I can see we have to take a ferry across the bay and to the large city. Sofia, Eugenia, and Claudia are close. Rond walks at my side, but not too close this time.

"Great-Aunt Georgia and my grandmother took a ferry from here to England," I say to my friends. "Grandma Pat didn't like the voyage too much, seasick the whole time." The others look to the choppy water and seem to understand.

"You take bus, yes?" Rond says and looks at me as he walks and tries to sort out what I'm talking about.

"Yes. Pamplona is inland from here," says Eugenia.

"Ah, I see," he says, then smiles as the pieces come together in his mind.

We follow many footprints in the sand, splash through puddles, and slide on slippery rocks along our way to the ferry. The cold, salty, aromatic sea air, wet sand, and fragrances of seaweed exposed at low tide wake me more than this morning's *té negro*. This thought makes my stomach growl.

"I'm getting hungry too," says Sofia from my left. I turn to see her smile grow.

I turn to Rond. He smiles. This is nice to see. I wish I had . . . wish we had talked things out before, back in Deba where we met, or soon after.

In Playa De Somo we find a bar and stop for café con leche and a bite to eat. Afterward, we walk through the touristy village to the embarcadero to catch a ferry to Santander. The wait is short and the ride across rough waters is long. I think I have my grandmother's genetics when it comes to crafts plying through rough waters. It helps to gaze at the city and shoreline as we approach. Compared to the little villages we have visited, this metropolis stretches far to the left and the right. I can see a mix of old and new. Spires of old churches and ultra-modern architecture speckle the cityscape.

Rond leans against the wide rim of the boat's bow, which goes up and down on the white-capped water far too much for my liking. He has his arms out wide, hands planted on the rails. His poncho flutters to one side, the stiff wind this morning coming from the north, off the Atlantic. He looks deep in thought, or deep in the moment.

"Can we go with you to the bus station?" asks Eugenia as she takes a seat beside me.

"If you would like. I bought my ticket this morning, before breakfast," I say as I hold up my phone. "All I need to do is find the station and the right bus, I guess." I wish I sounded more confident. I would like it if they did come along.

"Yes, we would like to see you off," she says with the request still there.

"Oh, yeah, I'd love for you to come with me," I say as the ferry bumps down from a big wave. My guts tighten and the world spins a little. I grasp the seat below me. Eugenia holds a warm smile. The boat shudders and climbs another large wave. I close my eyes and try not to imagine twenty-four hours of this during a crossing to England. How did my grandmother do it? How soon can we get to Santander?

Finally, we arrive at the port and return to land. The city buzzes with activity. The stark contrast to the last few days, the thought of leaving my new friends and hunting for a bus station, has my jaw muscles in clinch mode. The Germans, Cheng, and

Rond follow me as I guide them along a route to the bus station shown on my phone. It's an easy ten-minute walk. The bus company I have booked with has the first few bays as we enter the station.

We stand before a list of departures displayed on a large screen. My bus isn't here yet; departure is scheduled a half an hour from now. We huddle and chat like other groups in the station. Huge buses come and go. Passengers load and unload.

Claudia comes over, the first to give me a hug. We exchange phone numbers and in unison declare we will stay in touch. Sofia and Eugenia hug me at the same time. I feel the burn of tears behind my eyes. We already have each other's contact information.

"We will see you in Santiago, okay?" says Eugenia.

Unable to use my voice, I nod.

"If we have time, we will all go to Finisterre, the ends of the earth," says Sofia. Cheng agrees with a nod of her head, her short, dark hair waving like she's in a shampoo ad.

I nod again.

They step away. Rond comes over. I sense the others move away and can hear them pleasantly chattering with each other.

"Will I see you in Santiago, Rond?"

"I think maybe yes," he says. The way he talks makes me smile. I had trouble with it when we first met, but his speaking now warms me inside. I can never truly understand his past, his life in Oslo. He cannot fully understand my past. But we can now like each other because we can relate in some way. We've each had a rough start to life. That's what my grandmother said of me. She also said we should always seek a better way, a better path. And I believe Rond and I are doing that, which makes us closer, equals, friends.

I take a piece of folded paper from my pocket and give it to him. "It's my phone number."

He smiles a broad smile and says, "I text you."

Memories flood in like drapes that have been lifted to show a movie screen. He is odd; me too. I can see him sitting on a rock wall waiting for me. I recall the scene of him disappearing over a hilltop, us trying to determine what he was up to. I remember learning about his mother and sharing with him my past. I might never think of Rond as a boyfriend, but we are friends, even close friends. "I look forward to hearing from you."

A bus pulls into the bay nearest to us. Our Camino family gathers again. The placard on the front of the bus changes to Pamplona. Claudia hugs me again. Eugenia gives me a kiss on each cheek, Sofia the same. Rond takes my hands and smiles a tight smile. His brightly colored curls begin to quiver ever so gently, he lets me go, and walks away.

I find my seat on the bus, stow my pack in the overhead rack, and sit by the window. From here I can see them go. In a few minutes the bus departs and makes its way through the narrow streets of the city. Down a wider street, the bus passes my friends. I place a palm to the window, push my face close and watch them as we pass. Rond leads, looks at his phone, then up, and points out a turn at the correct corner. I smile.

The bus crawls through the city streets, finds a freeway, and circles around the bay, before reaching the countryside. Eventually, we turn inland, climb into forested hill country, and pass by vast vineyards.

Our bus delivers us to Pamplona, a city of nearly two hundred thousand humans. We have arrived in drier environments. The rolling hills outside the city are golden brown; *a short ride to California,* I jest to myself.

The bus comes to a stop beside a new station in the city center. I pull my backpack down and step into the line of people getting off. In the bright sun I sense the dry air and aromas, different smells than on the coast, less inviting.

I find a bench, pull out my phone, and dig for the name and number of Father Ernesto's friend. I poke at the digits and wait.

After several rings a woman picks up the phone and says, "Catedral." The one word greeting catches me off guard.

My palm sweats. "Hola. Está el Padre Emil ahí, por favor?" I grip hard on the smartphone yet worry it will squirt from my hand like a banana from its peel.

"Yes. Wait please," the woman says.

She has changed to English; my accent is worse than I thought.

After a few moments a man's voice comes on the line. "Father Emil."

"Yes, Father, my name is Summer Darling. Father Ernesto of the Buen Pastor in San Sebastián said I should call you when I arrive in Pamplona."

"Yes, yes, my child. Our Father Ernesto has called to me."

Here we go again with the "my child" tagline.

"My good friend Ernesto asks me to assist you if you like," Emil says.

"Are you at the Cathedral here in Pamplona?"

"Sí. Yes, the Catedral de Pamplona," he says. "You can take taxi to here. We know of place for you to stay if you like. I can give you guided tour of our cathedral, also."

I can only hope the place he mentions is as nice as the Pensión Ortiz in San Sebastián. "Está bien. I will see you soon. Gracias, Father Emil."

Pamplona, Spain
August 21, 1982

Patricia and I were here last month, but the city is so different now that the festival of San Fermín has passed by until next year. We didn't spend much time touring the old city, and I don't want to take the time now. I will search for any sign of our father, then move on.

From Georgia's Travel Journal

SEVENTEEN

Pamplona, October 15, 2019

The slamming of a door down the hall from my room wakes me before the dark, quiet city.

The outdoors call to me. I get up, pull on the warmth of my hoodie, and move to the window overlooking a plaza below. Opening the window, I feel a chill in the dry air and catch the unpleasant smells of stale beer and trash. Thankfully, from here I can see a sliver of the countryside, a rare treat this deep in the old city center.

Father Emil's sister owns this guest house, the Pensión El Camino. It's within walking distance to the Cathedral and not far off the Camino as it snakes its way through Pamplona.

Decision point: I could rest for a day, see more of the city as the padre had suggested. Or I could go as fast as my legs will take me.

Yesterday, Father Emil gave me a guided tour of his cathedral. He had pointed out the five-hundred-year-old gothic design. Only five hundred years. It replaced an older, Romanesque church, he said. What impressed me the most was how big and grand the cathedral was inside, in comparison to the narrow view of the façade from the small plaza out front. The place echoed with Emil's voice and the squeals of delight I imagined from Georgia as her presence followed us on our tour.

After our tour, and assuring Father Emil—and by extension Father Ernesto—that I am doing fine and my Camino experience has been better than I could have imagined, I took to the city streets. As I left him, I could see the concern in the old man's eyes. He would soon call his old friend in San Sebastián.

Sitting on a park bench, I had downloaded a city tour map onto my phone.

Following the tourist guide, distracted from the busy city around me, I learned of the week-long festival of *Sanfermines* each summer and of Ernest Hemingway's time here. I could see the pride this beautiful city has for its history and its traditions. Cafés, bars, and grand restaurants occupy many of the narrow streets and old-world plazas. I could also imagine my grandmother and her big sister here, not noticing the time, the decades since their last visit. Georgia closely eyeing the Spanish men, her sister shaking her head.

These thoughts of yesterday float through my mind and then fade away as the new day breaks.

I watch from my perch on the windowsill as crews of burly men in green uniforms with yellow stripes clean the plaza and streets with machine, power hose, and broom. They sparkle. The streets, I mean. They and the plaza are mostly made from square-cut stone. The stone shows its age, worn from use and regular cleaning. Every July, descendants of bulls my grandmother and great-aunt had watched in the 1980s run through these narrow streets. I'm okay with missing it, the spectacle of it, the crowds.

Now, right this minute, I think I've seen enough of Pamplona.

In a few minutes, I am dressed, and my backpack nearly ready to go. I check one more time on the journal, my passport, and Grandma Pat's debit and credit cards, safe in a pouch in my pack. I buckle down the top flap and look around the room again. Next, I slip on my puffy jacket, and then the backpack. Time to go.

The city streets slowly come to life. Restaurant and café owners rearrange tables and chairs, raise colorful umbrellas, and prop up today's menu, the *menu del día*, near their doors. Before I'm out of the city, I find a café con leche and a hot slice of Spanish tortilla. They are both delicious. I could get used to coffee this way. Or I already have.

Yesterday morning, while taking advantage of time and free Wi-Fi on the bus, I had downloaded an app for the Camino Francés. Today's trek has already started, and I still have no plan. I slide a finger over the screen of my phone, scrolling to my location in Pamplona. The math, easy for most people, takes forever to calculate in my mind. Finally sorted, I find a village on the map twenty miles from where I am. *Get on with it, girl.*

Once again, I find yellow arrows and head toward Santiago. A few other peregrinos, hike along up ahead. They stream out like soldiers on the march.

We hike quietly out of the city. The Camino snakes through rolling hills. A ridge line with wind turbines on top reaches toward the sky, six miles ahead. That is the Alto del Perdón I have read about, and today's highest point.

I come upon a woman with a flag pinned to her backpack and flapping in the breeze. The bit of dark blue material has a British flag in one corner and white stars in a pattern clearly symbolizing something to its people. "Buen Camino," I say as I match strides with her.

"Isn't it though," she says. "Don't you love these wide-open spaces?" Her accent sounds Australian.

I look around again, taking in as much as I can. "All of this space makes my heart soar."

She smiles.

The trail, now a rough double-track, steepens, reminding me of my trekking poles. They snap into place and fit comfortably into my palms, familiar. I listen to the Australian as we walk, and I move on when she says she needs to slow down.

We pilgrims are spread out now. I can see people high above and several well behind. The air feels dry, but I pull it in, happy and greedy as ever.

Warm, I decide to stop soon to take off my puffy. At the top of a short steep section the path flattens. Ahead, I see a lone, scraggly tree, a wooden bench beneath it, and a cute guy. "Buen Camino," I mumble as I near the spot.

"Buen Camino," he says. He's eating something, his backpack leaning against his legs.

I stop at the bench, set my poles down, and take off my backpack and jacket.

"Naranja?" he asks as he extends a hand full of the dripping fruit.

I hesitate for a long moment, then say, "Sí. Gracias." I take some of the offered orange segments and suck away the juice. Almost as a pig to slop, I gulp down the citrus goodness. It is so delicious, so perfect. And so is he. I look up and into his dark brown eyes. He looks to me with a broad smile and brilliant white teeth. He's gorgeous.

"A donde va, hoy?" he asks. It's a question, I can tell by the tone, but my mind—the part which supposedly does my translating—has gone elsewhere. "Where do you go today?"

"Ah, sorry . . ." I stutter. "Hm, lo siento." My face burns, no doubt red as a beet. As I stuff my jacket into its home in my backpack I work on a reply. All I have managed is to tell him I'm sorry. What am I sorry for? Being stupid? Being lousy at speaking the Spanish language, his language? Or I'm sorry I can't take him in my arms and ask him to kiss me, right here, right now?

"I walk to Puente la Reina today," he says.

"Ah, yeah, Queen's Bridge," I say.

He grins at my translation. Oh, sure, now it works. Well, it's not my translation, I read it in Georgia's journal. He's so cute. The dark curls, his honey-brown skin, the obvious strength in his taut muscles.

"I . . . I." Will this girl from California form a stutter, one that will haunt her for life?

"Yo . . . Hoy, voy a Mañeru, hoy." I have said the Spanish word for today twice. In one blasted sentence.

He smiles, cleans his hands with a red bandanna, and then picks up his backpack. I pick up my pack.

"Vamos?" he asks. "We go?"

I hear voices coming up the trail. Looking back, we can see six or eight heads coming over the rise. They talk loudly, all at once. In German, I believe.

"Sí, vamos," I agree, and finally return his smile.

We walk on, trekking poles digging in, biting at the densely packed gravel. The path cuts at an angle across the slope. I can hear the turbines rotating in the wind and look up.

"Viento, siempre viento, aquí," he says. "Windy, always."

"Sí. Viento," I repeat as I look over to him. I don't think he's as old as I had first thought. Older than Rond, much too old for me, my grandmother would say. Not too much, Grandma Pat. Not too, too much. We continue, a dozen questions for him come to mind. I don't ask a one.

In our silence, we have come to the top of our climb. On the large flat area are dozens of pilgrims and many tourists. A few vendors line the paved road leading from a highway to the north. People pose near metal sculptures of ancient pilgrims all facing toward Santiago. Others relax, have a bite to eat or drink from water bottles. A petite lady in a baby-blue food trailer makes smoothies for her customers. *You are no longer on the Camino del Norte, Summer Darling.*

The German group arrives. Their voices fold in with the others. I step to the edge, take a few pictures, and soak in the view. I strap the trekking poles to my pack. With a water bottle in my hand, I turn to look for the handsome Spaniard. I don't see him. Like, I don't see him anywhere. What the hell?

I mingle, and I search for him. More people arrive. As expansive as the place is, as far as the views reach out, the world closes in on me. I feel every muscle in my back and neck tighten. It's not the backpack, but me, them, all these people. I make another sweep, looking for that gorgeous man. He is not here. Time for me to go. I didn't even get his name.

At the westerly edge, I can see other pilgrims diving off the paved road and heading down the Camino as it slopes away from the crowds. I follow.

In a few strides the trail becomes steeper, more rugged. Loose gravel covers our path. I look back one more time, hoping to see him—and fall on my ass.

Puente la Reina (Queen's Bridge), Spain
August 23, 1982
I found where my father had worked in Pamplona. I must follow a clue given to me there. The owner of the hotel where he had worked on a remodel project told me my father followed his then employer to another job here in Puente la Reina.

From Georgia's Travel Journal

EIGHTEEN

Alto del Perdón, October 15, 2019

A hand reaches under my arm and helps me to my feet.

A flush of embarrassment sweeps over me. I hope *he* is the one helping me, the beautiful Spaniard. Still looking to the ground to put off disappointment, I dust myself off.

"Are you okay?" It's a man's voice, an older, American man's voice.

I finally look toward him. "I'm fine. Thanks."

"It's pretty steep here. You might want to use your poles," he says as he nods toward the trekking poles strapped to the side of my backpack. He slowly lets my arm go, making sure I have solid footing, then walks ahead.

I stand there for a moment, dazed, rubbing my backside. I take in the views on this side of the Alto del Perdón. The air, littered with a haze of dust and anticipation, feels dry and warm.

Voices from behind me stir my silence. I pull at my trekking poles. My feet want to slip at each tentative step. It seems to take me forever to snap the poles together and bring them to use in my battle to stay upright. The voices fall away, probably dealing with their own struggles against gravity and loose rock.

A layer of crushed white stone has been spread upon the trail. Someone had good intentions, but the gravel is so loose I'm not sure they have improved the pilgrims' progress. On the coastal route I enjoyed the sun, but here it attacks my bare skin. Reflecting off this white top-layer, those rays burn my eyes and sear my face. I start to walk.

The loose gravel ends. Thankfully, the foe didn't last too long, and the slope levels somewhat. The rush of my fall eases and I pick up the pace. My legs are pleased with the work, my butt bruised. I try to set those useless thoughts aside.

So far, as I follow my family's history to an unfamiliar place, more sights, people, and experiences have filled my life than in all my years before coming to Spain. The Sea of Biscay, the Norte, the women I now call friends, Rond and I figuring out how to become friends, the wonderful food and albergues. So many nice people.

Though this trail, the Camino Francés, looks different, I know I can do this.

Confidence is a good thing—until you fall and bruise your butt. The plan was to walk to Santiago de Compostela in the northwest corner of this country. For me it was that and being with the person I loved more than anyone else. I also wanted to learn about this country, see a new world in what we call the old world. After she died, and after Tilly came and went, I made new plans. Sure, I based them on the old ones, but I had to make them and stick to them—until I couldn't. Sometimes you develop a blister, or sleep on a couch, or you fall. And you get up. I can always get up.

But here comes the hard part: The American who helped me from my fall has stopped ahead. He's standing with a woman. They have stopped under a short shade tree drawing water from bladders in their packs. I will make myself talk with them.

"Buen Camino," the woman says.

"Buen Camino." I repeat, stopping a step or two beyond the shade of their tree. "Thank you for helping me back there," I say to the man.

The woman looks to him. He glances at her. "She took a spill back there, right after the summit."

She smiles. "Howard loves to help." They both wear wedding bands, so I assume they are married.

I want to say more, but don't. I want to ask them where they come from, the usual things. Mostly, I want to know if they have seen my beautiful Spaniard. I flush with the thought and turn to go.

"Where in the States do you come from?" he asks.

I turn back. "California."

Howard, a tall, athletic looking man, takes off his ball cap and sweeps sweat from his brow. He has short gray hair. The hairs on top of his head stand straight up.

They both look back up the trail. "Are you by yourself?" the woman asks, a motherly tone in her voice.

I'm a veteran of the Camino; of course I'm by myself. But then, I remember why.

"Yes, but no. I have met many wonderful, kind people," I say as I nod my head toward Howard, who drops his head a little. "I started the Camino Francés this morning, in Pamplona. I hiked on the del Norte before today."

"Oh, did you like the Norte? Howie and I would love to walk the north coast. Our next Camino, possibly," she says. "I'm Beth, by the way."

Beth, shorter than Howard seems fit, as well. Her curly dark hair has a few threads of white and gray.

"Hello. My name is Summer." The three of us begin walking again. "The coast was pretty, and green, and very moist, humid in comparison to here."

Beth nods her head and looks over. "Did you like the cities?"

I consider Beth's question for a long moment. The air around us has stalled, frozen in place. All I hear are our six footsteps crunching in the gravel path. "I guess I've confirmed I am a country girl. I spent too much time in San Sebastián, passed by Bilbao as fast as possible, and caught a bus out of Santander."

"Then you love this wide-open space?" says Howard as he opens his hands wide, his trekking poles hanging from their straps.

"Oh, yes. I could breathe it all in." They both smile at my delight.

"Where will you stop tonight?" asks Beth.

"I had planned on Mañeru." *His* beautiful, tanned face and dark curls flood my mind's eye. "But I may stop in Puente la Reina." A short day for me. I may find him. Or I could use the time to reread more of Georgia's journal.

We are on gravel roads with wide-open fields on both sides. The path is mostly level. We walk along chatting about home. They are from Colorado, both retired from the military. This is Beth and Howard's second Camino, both on this route.

"Why do people come back, do the Camino again?" I ask from nowhere, with nowhere in mind. The idea of coming back, of returning to the Camino, has never eased its way into my thoughts. Not until now.

"They say the Camino gets into your blood," says Howard, now beside me.

Beth walks slightly behind. "It certainly has gotten into ours.

At home we talk so much about the Camino our friends want to run away when we start retelling our stories."

"Do you keep a journal?" I ask.

"Howie does. He's good about keeping a record. I take the pictures, he writes it all down," Beth says. "How about you? Do people your age keep diaries?"

I sense something in her words; she's fishing for my age. "I don't know about other people. I probably should. Just never thought of it, somehow." The thought strikes me like a stick. Will I have a family one day? Will others want to read about what I have done here? Or will they think, *Who the hell walks across a whole country by themselves?*

We pass through a village. There's no one around. The streets are spotless. The Camino goes on; we don't stop. In a couple of kilometers another village appears. A group of people with backpacks have stopped at an intersection in the center of the village. We join them.

Howard and Beth know these people and they all start talking. I get introduced to the foursome: Cheryl, Scott, Yan, and Felipe. They all look like Camino veterans. Cheryl is as tall as I am, about ten years older, and has a warm smile. She's also from the States. Scott is English, has red hair and light skin, which now has patches of red sunburn. Yan is Danish, thin, and only as tall as Cheryl and I. During our introductions Felipe has twice inspected me from top to bottom, especially focusing on my chest. He's darkly tanned, short, and thickly built, with a pudgy face.

The group discusses a church not far from the Camino. They plan to walk the few miles to visit it. Howard and Beth seem eager to make the short bypass with them. They invite me along. "Since you changed your plans . . ." Howard says, a glint in his eyes.

I look for the next yellow arrow. A hundred feet away, a crude splash of paint lies on the corner of a rock wall. I have not once gone out of my way to see something off-route, to detour from Georgia's path. My goals are in the direction of the yellow paint. I could simply say my goodbyes and walk on. Tearing myself away from the thought, I pull around and face the open countryside and our bypass. "Sure, I'll go." This reply, which has slipped from my mouth, surprises me. But I'll go with it. I have the time. "Where are we going?"

"To the church at Eunate," says Felipe, as he slips close to my side as our group begins to walk. He has a leering gaze and a wide, wolfish grin on his face. I feel the afternoon heat weighing me down. Perspiration blooms. I pull the band of my hat down over my forehead to soak up the beads of sweat forming there.

Howard closes in. I'm about to scream or bolt or something when he says, "Eunate is a spiritual place." I glance toward him. He stares at Felipe, a hard warning in his gold-flecked dark brown eyes. "Historians know little about the history of the place, but many people have experienced a sort of spiritual sensation while visiting the church." Howard now looks to me, then back to the trail.

Felipe has eased a few inches away, but he's still too close for my liking.

"If you are into architecture, the church is Romanesque and considered one of the most interesting in Navarra."

Felipe closes in on me again. "Zee Pope would love this church in the middle of nowhere, if he could walk with us."

I glance at Howard as he gives Felipe another warning look. With a nod of his head, he directs the creep away from me. I feel like I'm between good and evil. Felipe is the type of man I have been around most often. Somehow, I know Howard is one of the good guys. He has a stern edge but a heart that will always want to help others.

I peek over my shoulder to the now retreating Felipe, then back to Howard. I let out a long sigh.

"Don't pay him any attention. He thinks all women want him," says Howard.

We walk along in pairs and trios, each conversing about different things. In the middle of the vast open landscape surrounded by rolling hills, we find the church. There are a few other pilgrims milling about, taking pictures, some lying on the grass. As we enter the grounds, a carload of Spanish tourists pulls into the gravel parking lot. They all get out.

Eunate is a quiet, peaceful place in the middle of nowhere. The stone used to build the structure has the same golden shade of gray as the sunburned stalks of corn in the fields behind the ancient, eight-sided building.

Tourists and pilgrims, both, walk about calmly, their voices not more than whispers. It's like they all try to feel the energy, the something special here, yet are disappointed they have not. I slip away from the groups, collapsing my poles and strapping them onto my pack. I enter the church, but only a step or two inside the door. My shoulders are bare. I should have worn my long-sleeved sun shirt today. I take a couple of pictures in honor of my grandmother and her sister and return to the sunlit outdoors. Howard and Beth come up behind me.

"They say," Howard begins, "if you take off your shoes and slowly walk around the church three times, you will experience the powers of this place." The two of them step through the doors and into the church.

Outside again, I move to one side of the building to find a quiet place to lie down for a few minutes. Surrounding the odd, octagon shaped church is a cobblestone walkway and an open colonnade topped with arches. Beyond that a short distance is another wall, which is not quite as tall as me. A scraggily lawn fills the few yards between the walls. At my chosen spot, I drop my pack and lie down on the grass. I can hear hushed voices now and again, the rustle of cornstalks beyond the wall, and birds chirping. A slight breeze floats through occasionally and I catch the scent of some sort of sweet flower in the dry air.

A calmness takes over, but before I make the mistake of lying down completely and falling asleep, I sit up and take off my shoes. A couple, the woman holding a toddler on her hip, slowly, wordlessly pass me by. Before I have my shoes off, the couple has gone. I stand, set my shoes on my pack, and begin the first of three loops.

I slowly count three rounds of the church and sit back down at my backpack to put my shoes on. The thought of that horrible deed makes me cringe. Delaying the inevitable, I pull my socks off to perform a thorough inspection. The few red spots and the big toe, once mangled by a huge blister, remain securely encased under new applications of gauze and tape.

Hearing my group at the entrance, it sounds like they are preparing to return to the Camino. Beth comes my way. "We're leaving soon," she says.

"I'll catch up to you," I say.

Puente la Reina, Spain
August 25, 1982
Stayed here in Queen's Bridge for an extra day. Spent my time in search of work my father had done here, projects he worked on. I also found another woman who very clearly remembered him, a twinkle in her eye, I thought. She reluctantly said father's employer returned to Pamplona and father walked the Camino out of town and toward Santiago.

From Georgia's Travel Journal

NINETEEN

Eunate, October 15, 2019

Beth has returned to the group, and I hear their voices fade away. I slip my angry feet into socks and shoes. I don't feel anything special, no spirit taking over, or any inspirational words from God.

What do you know of God, Laura? My mother once tried to invoke God on me. She ran me down as I tried to run away from her. She—very surprisingly—caught up to me, cut me off. When I stopped, she thanked God. I had never heard my mother, or my father, mention the divine before then. Not once. I was mad, and she wanted to talk about it, talk about what Paul was. To get her to drop the subject, I taunted her, used her words against her. What did she know of God? My memory of her now pulls at my heart. How are Adam and Laura? How is my mother handling the death of her mother? She should know by now. I tighten the straps of my backpack and turn to walk back to the road, wishing to leave those thoughts behind for a while longer.

I see the trail and move in that direction. A calm takes over my body, muscles relax.

As though carried on a stiff breeze, I feel weightless. I glide across the grass. The church sweeps past. My legs are moving, I know they are. But I don't feel the effort, don't feel sore feet touching the dirt path I have come to. My arms fold across my chest. What's happening? I'm now on the single-track path. I can see Howard and Beth and the rest of the group not far ahead, slightly out of focus. A multi-layered glow surrounds each of them, even Felipe.

My progress feels effortless, a delightful tune buzzing in my head, my feet happy, pain-free. What the heck? Is this what Howard meant? Focus slips away.

Everything around me glows in a murky, out-of-focus rush past the windows that are my eyes. It's like I'm on a ride, in a vehicle, zooming along, but slowly. I bring my blurred awareness to a point inside. Every blood vessel and capillary thrums with the flow of their purpose. Each muscle relaxes further, doing their work but without struggle. My heart pumps in slow rhythm, like walking isn't any kind of real work. It feels like I'm sliding, rolling on skates, pushed by a huge sail on a tiny breeze. Farther down the trail I come to another farm road. Without the tiniest thought of it, I make the correct turn and follow the others.

I can hear their conversations from up ahead. I don't want to catch them. I don't really want to hear their words. Or are these their thoughts? It's hard to tell.

The countryside glides by, but I don't notice, don't fully absorb its passing. Tall grasses and short bushes flow together on a gentle breeze. I don't feel this; it's too beyond—outside whatever I'm going through. But inside, in the shell, there's a scent, something familiar but not quite. Something clean and pungent, but soothing.

We return to the official Camino path, popping out from our detour to Eunate on the outskirts of Puente la Reina. The others have stopped. They are waiting for me. I stop, focus on returning, my awareness rejoining the physical me. A large church stands beside us, and the Camino, leading to the main street, stretches out in front of us.

"Felipe and Yan want to stay there," says Beth to me as she points at the church. "We're going to an albergue we liked before, during our last Camino. It's in the center of town. How about you?"

It's then, when she addresses me, that everything comes to final, brilliant life. I feel myself again, my new self. My feet have actual contact with the ground. "Did you feel that?" I ask.

"Feel what?" asks Howard, a knowing smile on his face.

Felipe and Yan are not interested and say their goodbyes. They head toward the old church.

Beth comes close. "Are you okay?"

"Oh, yeah. Um, I'm fine," I say. "It's just . . ." I have no idea how to explain my experience. "Yeah, I'll go with you, stay where you stay."

Cheryl and Scott lead. As we walk through town, I try, unsuccessfully, to let go of whatever *it* was.

I step close to Howard. He looks over. "Thank you for that," I say.

"Sure thing. We could talk about it later, share our thoughts," he says.

Right now, I just want to let the feeling soak in. But I do want to talk with him, hear of his experience at an oddly shaped church in the middle of nowhere.

More and more pilgrims come into view as we enter the

center of town. Realizing this, I do a quick search for my handsome Spaniard. His lovely face is not among the others.

We stop at an albergue. Howard checks inside and says they have enough beds for us for the night. We queue up, starting the check-in process.

I have drawn myself into a shell, thoughts of Georgia competing with memories of the day: my first day on the Camino Francés, the young, handsome Spaniard, and the experience I had after Eunate. And a desire to eventually talk about it, another new happening in my life.

After cleaning up, I find Howard in the rectangular courtyard. He sits at a plastic table with a scraggly, almost leafless tree beside him. The sun falls low, casting long shadows. A thin layer of smoke from a wood fire rolls over the buildings and fills the space. The vapor contains the scents of roasting peppers, a warm, nutty fragrance, these followed by garlic smelling so delicious I can almost see it sizzling in olive oil.

Howard sips on a beer. When he sees me, he waves me over. I sit. A few people hang out their clothes to dry and chat with each other.

"Want to tell me about it?" he asks, his eyes trying their best to read me, to see if I'm ready.

"I don't know how to describe what happened." I hesitate, hoping the words will come. And they do. They pop out from nowhere and everywhere. "It was all energy, like nothing more than positive energy. All the good in the universe carrying me along, showing me the way," I say.

Howard sits forward. "Well, I think you've described it pretty well."

"Did you have the same feeling?"

"Yes. Something similar." He drops his head a little, seeming to relive the moment.

"When you and Beth came here for your first Camino?"

"Yes. Beth didn't have the same encounter as I did, but she believed what I told her later about mine. She has seen the difference in me since then."

He lifts his eyes to mine. I look at him quizzically, my head involuntarily tilting to one side.

"Summer, my team saw a lot of action in Iraq. This happened many years ago." He pauses for a moment, a ghostly white taking over his face. "I don't tell this story to many people, you understand?"

I nod, though I'm not sure I do.

"Our chopper got shot down. Most of the crew, my friends, were killed. Only two of us made it back to base that night. To say it was an ugly thing, to say we saw the darkness in our enemy, is an understatement."

He stops. I'm frozen. I couldn't say anything even if I knew what to say.

"The Camino was Beth's idea. Her mother ministers in a church. And like her, Beth always wants to help. I suppose that's why we came together. She hoped the things she'd read about the Camino, the healing powers, would help me. They did, of course. But what helped the most was my time at Eunate. Like you said, it was all the good in the universe. It picked me up and carried me and showed me the other side of darkness, to the light. 'It' fails as a word for the energy you and I have experienced. The spirit, an arm of God, perhaps, whatever *it* is, introduced me to my eye inside, my intuition, the part in the center of our chests we call heart."

His eyes are moist. He lowers his face and wipes his eyes with a sleeve.

"I don't know what to say, Howard. But I think I understand." He sits quietly and nods his head.

After a few moments, he looks to me and says, "We had better find Beth and then a pilgrim's menu."

My stomach churns in anticipation. I smile. "I'll catch up with you in a minute."

"Sure thing," says Howard as he gets up and goes in search of Beth.

Now alone, new thoughts want to consume me: *Did my great-grandfather find his way out of the darkness? Did people he met while walking this path share with him? And . . . What have I found? What more will I find? What will find me?*

Viana, Spain
August 27, 1982
The woman at the hostel where I stayed last night remembered Father. It seemed a fond memory, that she was attracted to him. She would only say, "He was a strong, lovely man."

From Georgia's Travel Journal

TWENTY

Viana, October 17, 2019

The Camino crosses a quiet highway then crosses it again. Along the path now behind me are endless fields, a few trees, and not much more. Ahead, Viana, a small city on the maps. I'm glad I'm here, though, because I need water. Last night, we had talked about this being a long day. It's a warm one too.

A car zooms past. Buildings sprout up from the brown earth as I come closer to town. Apartment complexes are the first sign of civilization I have seen in hours. A truck with a line of cars behind it rumbles by on the highway. As I enter the little city, the road squeezes down to narrow streets. Literally walls closing in, structures now reach over me from the edge of the sidewalks. I push away the feeling of tightness, a restriction in my chest.

I will find a water fountain in the center of town, along my route. I can see a church ahead.

Sure enough, in front of the church a fountain flows freely in the middle of a plaza. People stream from alleys and other streets into the plaza. Vender stalls are busy, and the tables and chairs of cafés are full of locals, tourists, and pilgrims.

I'll fill my bottles and get out of town as quickly as I can.

I've almost finished, slipping the last bottle into its net pouch at my side. I'm ready to turn and leave when I see Howard stroll into the plaza. He looks tired but sees me and smiles. I return the smile and wait for him.

"Hey. I need water too. Been sucking it down like crazy today."

"Is Beth with you?" I ask.

"No. She and Cheryl and Yan walk slow today. The gals—Sorry. Beth and Cheryl will talk, talk, talk. Who knows when we will see them again?"

I'm ready to go. Howard has his backpack off. He fills the bladder inside with fresh water from the fountain and searches for something deep inside the pack. I pace about a little, then walk around the fountain like I'm seeking another spiritual experience. One I hope will transport me out of this town. A bus stops in one of the narrow streets, blocking traffic, and even more people file out and flow into the square.

I can see my exit, a dark alley. The one with a Camino scallop shell beside it on the corner of a building. I return to Howard's side to check on his progress.

"You okay, Summer?"

"Yeah, sure."

"I'm almost done, but you don't have to wait for me," he says.

"I'm okay waiting," I say as I slowly walk in a tight circle.

"You act like a trapped cat."

I stop my nervous pacing. "Sorry. I, uh, well. . ." I glance from face to face in the knots of people around us. "I don't like crowds. Thought I got better at it, but the peace of the Camino out there. . ." I wave a hand toward the space outside the city.

"Where the hell did it get to?" Howard fusses. After a moment he stops, looks up at me, and says, "So, last night. . ."

"Yeah."

"At the albergue, before dinner, you read something in the courtyard and then got up and left for a while. Looked like you were on a mission," he says, as he returns to his search. "None of my business. Just curious."

"You try to distract me," I say. Howard grins at me, digs around in his pack some more.

"Oh, to hell with it," he finally says in disgust, and closes the cover of his pack and cinches the cord. He throws the backpack over his shoulders and snaps the buckles.

"It surprises me, this feeling," I say to him. "It's like being squeezed by one of those huge snakes from the jungle. We went from nothing more than open fields and a few trees to this." My limp hand waves about again.

His eyes follow my gesture and my meaning. "Let's get you out of here. Nice place to visit, but we've got places to go," he says with a kind smile.

We come to the dark alley I had been eyeing and follow the Camino markers to the edge of Viana. As sudden as our entrance into the city, we leave it behind. "A blip on the radar," says Howard out of the blue. The question in my mind covers my face. "The place is only a memory now, behind us. I'm not a psychiatrist. But if I tried to help you, I'd say something like that. It's a blip in your day."

"Thanks," I say.

"I would also say it's damn hot today. Beth suggested we do this Camino in October. '"The weather is nice and cool in October,' she said. Ha." Then he throws his hands up and curses under his breath. "Now I remember where it is." He unzips a pouch on the side of his pack, pulls out a ball cap, and slips it on his head. "Better."

We walk along for a while without saying much. The expanse around us opens the space within me. I relax.

"So, last night, I'm still curious, I guess," says Howard up ahead of me on the narrow gravel trail.

"It's a long story." He doesn't respond. "Hmm, well, I have a journal my great-aunt wrote while on Camino decades ago."

"Really? How cool," he says.

"There's more, though. She searched for her father. He came to Spain, left his family behind, when she was little. She—and her sisters—they called him their 'wayward father'."

"Why did he leave home?"

"You see, that's the interesting part. Well, it's interesting to me, now. After you talked about your time in Iraq, I went back to try and understand more of my great-grandfather's story. All Aunt Georgia and her sister Patricia knew was that he had fought in Vietnam and when he returned home, he couldn't handle the pressure, so he left. They heard rumors he went to Spain and might have walked the Camino de Santiago. The family didn't know a thing about the Camino, not then. Not many people did, I suppose." Howard turns his head to look at me over his shoulder. There is interest, compassion, and empathy on his face.

"My time at Eunate . . . after . . ." I search for the right words and focus on my steps as they crunch on loose gravel. "And your story, your description of the darkness. It all made sense, somehow. Your words told me part of my great-grandfather's story. Or, at least, filled in some gaps."

Damn. I knew this would happen. That as soon as I started to talk about the past, the words would flow. *Careful.*

"Where did you go last night, though?"

Do you trust this man?

Why *do* I trust this man? "Aunt Georgia's journal said her father had worked in Monjardín. He did some restoration work on the church. I went to see what I could find. You know, possibly see his initials in the mortar or chiseled into a stone."

"And did you find anything?"

"No. I felt him, though, felt them. He and my great-aunt Georgia." *And my Grandma Pat,* I keep to myself. As I recall yesterday, goosebumps rise on my warm skin.

"How did it feel?" asks Howard.

"Like being in a living room with all the people who love you. That's it . . . love. And I could almost see, though not quite focus on them." Howard has stopped in front of me and turned to listen. "Do you ever have such feelings?" I ask as I look into his eyes.

"Not a strong awareness, like I know who is there, but yes. You see, I don't have any family, no blood relations. I was adopted," Howard says. "And Beth and I got too busy with our careers to ever want children."

"It felt so different, but I wasn't afraid," I say.

"Have you often experienced such . . . what do we call them? Visions?" he asks.

"Not before our time at the odd church. It's like it opened a door to something . . . I don't know. Something special."

We start walking again. Since the previous town, our walk has been easy, descending toward a river. Now the Camino arrows guide us through flat, hot farmland. We continue without speaking for a long while. So long, I wonder what he's thinking. It's then that I hear his heavy breaths and see his slumped shoulders, both very uncharacteristic of this warrior.

"There are no trees, no shade out here. And it's so horribly hot," Howard says and stops where our dirt track comes to a highway. "Since my time in the Middle East, I don't like the heat, the sun beating down on me."

We start walking again, slower, crossing the paved road, and following an arrow to a double-track path between freshly tilled fields. The Camino leaves the highway behind. We can no longer hear the occasional rush of cars or trucks. I notice another change: Vineyards stretch out in every direction.

Howard sees this too. "We are coming into La Rioja, a world-famous wine region."

In the distance, Howard sees a church, miles from anything, in a grove of trees. The idea of resting in the shade for a bit quickens his step. Picnic tables sit under the tree in front of the church. They pull us from the trail.

"Aaaahhh," says Howard in a long, drawn-out syllable of joy.

I happily agree with him.

I find a nut bar to snack on and sip from my water bottle. Howard wipes sweat from his brow and lies back on a bench made of concrete, grumbling the whole time about how hot it is and how he's going to point out this fact to Beth as soon as he sees her again.

Stretched out on my table I say, "You know the journal I was telling you about?"

"Yeah," he says from under the hat now covering his face, his voice almost too low for me to hear.

"Their time started in France. Aunt Georgia and her sister Patricia traveled through parts of Europe that summer. Georgia had been on other trips, but it was Pat's . . . Patricia's very first trip. She had just graduated from high school."

"Is that why you came to trek across Spain?" Howard asks, with more energy this time.

"Um, yes, I suppose." I have to remember he thinks I'm eighteen and probably recently graduated myself.

"They did all kinds of things. Stayed at a chateau with some girls they had met, saw the running of the bulls in Pamplona, slept on beaches. They even caught a ride with some drug smugglers one time."

Howard sits up and sets his cap on top of his pack. He gives me a look. I'm not quite sure what it means.

"Now who tries to distract whom?" he says with a broad smile.

I grin.

"What?" asks Howard.

"That makes me think of my cousin Louise. She laughs every time she hears the word 'whom.'"

We're having a good laugh when we hear voices coming in our direction. Beth leads, Cheryl and Yan right behind her. "What's so funny?"

"You," says Howard with a bitter tone to his words but a grin on his face.

"Is he going to bitch about it being too hot?" she says to me as she gives him a quick kiss.

They start chatting, Beth trying to hug her husband, him still complaining about the heat.

My thoughts return to Georgia's journal. And how I don't know the ending.

Logroño, Spain
August 29, 1982

Oh my, it's hot here. One would think you would become accustomed to this Spanish heat. I think it becomes worse each day. The locals . . . well, the lady who owns the hostel I'm staying in, says the days have been hotter than normal this year. I'll bet. Father must have experienced the summer as he followed work through this region.

From Georgia's Travel Journal

TWENTY-ONE

Logroño, October 18, 2019

Air conditioning would feel good right about now.

Howard had brought the subject up again as we walked into town. He wanted to get a room at a nice hotel and "enjoy modern conveniences." As we cross the river, Beth scoffs at the idea, says there's a perfectly suitable albergue around the corner and on the main street, close to cafés and shops.

"Can you imagine how hot it gets here during the summer months?" I say, teasing Howard. The rest of the group assents.

"This has been the warmest day since I arrived in Spain," says Cheryl. The group agrees.

At Beth's chosen albergue, we find the doors locked. We are too early. A sign on the door indicates they will open in half an hour. This is common, the others tell me. They all remove their packs, lean them against a wall of alabaster colored stone, and sit down to wait.

Should I go on?

"It's only half an hour," says Beth, as I stand there undecided.

"I think I'll go to that café," I say as I point across the wide street. "I should check on things back home." The others let me go; they have settled in for a well-earned rest.

The server, in crisp white shirt and black vest, opens a large red umbrella to shade me and my table. He takes my order. I ask for the Wi-Fi password. He scribbles it on a scrap of paper, hands it to me, and slips away. I'm happy for the shade. The streets are quiet, siesta time. A thinly built dog strolls past in a lazy weave among the tables then saunters near to the pilgrims across the street, looking for a handout.

My soda arrives, accompanied by a semi-transparent glass filled to the top with glorious ice cubes. I open my backpack and throw back the top cover to expose Georgia's journal pages. As my phone negotiates with an internet connection, I pull out her diary. I spread out the pages, hoping to better understand the mystery. So far, I have read Grandma Pat's sister was on their father's "scent" (her word). She had found someone who knew him when he worked in Pamplona five years before. From there, he walked to Puente la Reina. I had found the place he worked on during his time there. It was an albergue at the time, but closed and broken down now, decades later.

"Do you mind, Summer?"

It's Beth. "No, please . . . sit," I say as I pull my things in.

"What have you got there?" she asks.

I don't respond and don't know why.

"Howie told me a little about your family, about your aunt's journal," she asks with a nod toward the papers in front of me.

I glance toward Howard across the street. He's stretched out again, the ball cap over his eyes.

Beth looks uncomfortable now, sitting on the edge of her chair. The waiter appears. She hesitates, but finally orders a soda and a bag of chips. Which sounds really good. I order a bag of my own.

"Sorry for asking about your things. That was rude of me," says Beth.

"No, no. I'm sorry. It's not a problem. Only I . . . I haven't talked much about her journal before today."

Beth sits there quietly, waiting for me to spill my guts.

My phone finally connects, and a series of vibrations indicate several messages wait for my attention. I only know two people at home and a few more here in Spain who have internet access and use it. Some of those people are across the street, leaning against a stone wall, napping.

The waiter brings out Beth's soda. Her smile grows wide as she pours her lemon soda over ice. She sips a bit of the cold liquid, then sits back into her seat, contented.

There are several texts from Lou, an email from Lou with an attachment, and a handful of messages on WhatsApp from my Camino del Norte family. They make good progress, it seems. I'll have to look at a map to know for sure. I'll do that later.

Lou's first message is just her checking on me. It's a couple of days old.

But the second one quickly steals all my attention.

Another package from Astorga, Spain, came in the mail today.

She knows now to send it to me right away. The next message says she has.

Scanned it and sent with an email.

I glance at the next few messages, Lou wanting to know if I received her email.

I fumble with the phone and its virtual buttons, both attempting to escape my sweaty palms and damp fingers. Beth watches my every move with curiosity. I stay on task.

Finally, I get the email open and immediately open the scanned document. I scroll through about twenty pages of Georgia's familiar handwriting. Lou has added a line of her own at the bottom of the last page.

Summer, this is not the end of the journal. It's cut off.

I can see that. I return to the cover page, a note written in Spanish. The scanned page is on the same kind of note paper as before.

¿Vendrás a buscar a tu familia? (Will you come to find your family?)

I sit back, stunned. Find my family?

Beth has finished her soda. Ready to return to the albergue, she toys with a pile of Euro coins, selecting the correct amount. She slides them toward me and starts to get up.

"Howard told you my great-aunt Georgia kept a Camino diary," I say while aligning the pages and returning them to their plastic sleeve. Beth sits back, hoping I continue. I don't.

She can't take it any longer. "That's fantastic. When did she walk the Camino?"

"1982."

"Oh my," Beth says as she leans forward. "And you brought it along to read as you walk the Way?" she says as she points a lithe finger toward the papers.

I nod my head. I'm still not sure how deep into my family's history I want to take another person. I'm afraid if I start talking again, everything will come flying out, splattering on the table and street and the magnificent old buildings near us. I might tell her about Grandma Pat dying, about Tilly coming to Spain, of me leaving her to deal with her sister's body, about my true age.

"It's okay, I understand," says Beth.

"No, I . . ." The words don't come to me. They are blocked by my past, my fears, my Grandma Pat. She probably would have told Beth to mind her own damn business. But that's not in me. I know this now. I look up, then across the street, stalling.

And there he is, making the last few steps to the albergue. I have no idea if my mouth has flown open, if I'm drooling, or my eyes have bugged out.

"What?" Beth turns to follow my gaze. "Oh, isn't he just . . ."

Yes, he is. The Spaniard from Alto del Perdón stands there, as gorgeous as I remember. He slips off his backpack, ready to take a position in the line for a bed tonight. He sees me, a smile spreads across his face, and he gracefully reshoulders his pack.

Beth turns back to me. "Do you know him?"

"Um . . ." I'm going to stop right there, but I can't. "Hmm, not exactly."

"Hola," he says. "Hello." He turns to Beth and gives a slight bow. Oh, God, he bowed to her.

Beth's mouth is agape. She quickly gathers herself, murmurs a few words, and makes an excuse to go. "I'll be in line, Summer. We'll save you a bunk, okay?"

"Yes, that's super." *That's super?* What are you, five years old?

"May I sit?" he asks.

I simply wave a lazy hand over the seat beside me. He sits, tucking his backpack under the table.

"I lost you up there," I say, just as stupidly as, *that's super*.

"Ah, sí. I was sorry to . . . how do you say, to lose you?" He puts out a hand and says, "My name is Macario. It means Blessed."

Oh, yes, he is. I shake his hand ever so daintily with my damp hand. *Gross.* "My name is Summer. You know, like the season. Are you staying here tonight?" I ask dumbly.

"Yes, if they have room. I think they will for me, for all of us," he says as he glances to the pilgrims across the street. There is my group. Funny how fast they have become *mine*. More arrive. Some familiar faces, many very tired looking and sunburned. Which reminds me.

"I need to buy sunscreen this evening, after the shops reopen," I say.

"Hace color, hoy," he says.

My head bobbles. "Very hot, muy caliente."

The waiter comes to take Macario's order. Other pilgrims take their seats at nearby tables. Our server looks disappointed with the added workload. He writes down Macario's order for a soda on his little notepad and then goes to raise more umbrellas.

A sudden shift in activity across the street steals my attention away. The door to the albergue opens on squeaky old hinges. The line stands like a wave at a ballpark, and pilgrims slowly begin to shuffle inside.

"I should go. Will we see you later?"

"Ah, sí," says Macario as he turns to see what is happening. "Perhaps later we have la cena, have supper together?"

I try to lift my pack to go and nearly fall over when he asks his unnerving question. "Yes, great idea. I'll see if Howard and Beth want to join us."

He smiles a tight smile. He's disappointed with my plus-two. So am I.

Burgos, Spain
September 2, 1982

I telephoned mother a few days ago. I've been stewing about our conversation ever since. I told her I was on Father's trail, I had found some clues, people who knew him. She cried at first, then listened. So, I went on. She began to sob. Through racks of grief, she said for me to stop, she was so tired of still waiting for "that man to return," she'd had enough. Should I call it quits, leave his memory be? Should I go home?

From Georgia's Travel Journal

TWENTY-TWO

San Juan de Ortega, October 21, 2019

The gravel road I thought would never end finally comes to a village.

The sun hangs low, I'm beat, and as every hour goes by, I miss my friends more and more, especially the cute Spaniard. Cold air seeps into my sweaty clothes, feeling like I've stepped into a refrigerator. After a couple of blocks, I find a pensión. It's full for the night. Ugh. The twenty-six bones in each of my feet float on pillows of swollen flesh, plantar digital nerves tingling as if too close to a fire. I shouldn't have walked on, left the others wherever they have stopped for the night. It seemed like a good idea at the time.

The path through those countless miles of rolling terrain rolled along peacefully, though. I liked the solitude, and it would have been lonely if not for my great-aunt Georgia's and Grandma Pat's combined presence. They guided me through thoughts of home, family, and the Camino. In another time, my great-grandfather walked these same hills, through these forests where I once saw a badger and later the tail end of a deer-like creature. Aunt Georgia had ventured along the same line he trekked, and I have plodded.

I never met her, but I've seen pictures. There's one on the fireplace mantle at Grandma Pat's, Georgia standing in front of a cathedral. No surprise there. It was a massive white-stone building in Milan, Italy. After the journal arrived, my grandmother showed me pictures of the two of them at a party someplace in Europe. Georgia was tall and thin and beautiful, with long twisting curls of bombshell blond hair. And her eyes always spelled out *Let's Do This*, whatever *this* may have been at the time.

Right now, for me, all I want is a place to sit down. I come to a monastery, the largest building in this little town. A mix of Romanesque art and Gothic arches looms above me as I pass through iron gates to find the door with a sign for the albergue. I can hear voices from inside, dozens of them. The dark wood door under a tall arch stands open, and I stick my head in. A monk picks up his things at a desk inside the entrance. He is round, built like a snowman on sticks.

He looks up. "Completo," he says with severe finality.

Crap. They are full for the night. I've done it to myself again. Dammit.

A nearby bench calls me. I point to it and say, "Está bien?" He indicates I can, but he comes to stand in front of me as I gingerly take a seat.

"Estamos llenos por la noche." He has his arms wrapped

around a large ledger with a tattered binding, a stern, get-out-of-here look on his face. I want to cry.

"Summer, is that you?" It's Cheryl, with Yan at her side. She sees it's me, or what's left of me after this long—now ugly—day.

"How did you two beat me here? I thought you were behind," I say as they stride up with their showered cleanliness and well-rested appearance.

"Oh, we caught a ride. Then we took a cab. And then walked the last bit from Oca," says Cheryl.

Yan nods his head. "Like this," he says.

The monk has stalled out beside them. Cheryl turns to him. "Don't you have anything for our friend? Summer has walked a very long way today." The man in robes twists up his face, quizzical. Cheryl changes to a broken Spanish translation. His expression flattens. Then he perks up a bit.

"Summer?" he murmurs.

"Yeah, like the season. Verano. Sí?" says Cheryl.

"Espere aquí," he says, the ledger still tight to his chest. His gray robes float and flutter behind him as he walks away from us.

"He wants you to wait," says Cheryl.

"Yeah. But I'm curious. He seemed to take notice at the mention of my name."

"I saw that, too."

The old monk comes back in a moment, another one with him. This new monk, taller and younger, speaks some English. He is also more polite. He says they have a storage room where I can stay the night. But I have to register first.

The first monk and I go to his desk. He officiously records my passport number and slams their rubber stamp on my pilgrim credential and dates it. The other man leads us to a room not much larger than my closet at Grandma Pat's house. Both sides of the room are lined with sway-backed wooden shelves holding short stacks of white linens and wool blankets.

Even with a faint but horrid smell of chemicals—probably to ward off bedbugs—the space feels heavenly perfect.

Cheryl makes sure I'm okay with my strange accommodations and points out the direction to the showers. "We are in the courtyard. Find us when you get done. We can eat together," she adds.

I settle in and eventually get cleaned up.

At the communal dining table, we muse how the meal the monks served is far from the best the Camino has to offer. Agreement ripples along our table, then away from us, and to the other tables. Everyone in the room seems to have finished eating at the same time. The cacophony of voices lifts to a roar. From my closet to the shower, then my end of this table, I had kept the mass of humans at bay. But now, as the dozens upon dozens of pilgrims begin to clamor at once, I can no longer ignore their presence. The stone of the monastery absorbs some of the noise, but not enough. The contrast of this situation to the peace and quiet of the trail still shocks me.

There is a bar past the end of the monastery complex, at the edge of town. Yan wants to get a beer. Cheryl decides to go with him. I don't think it was a difficult decision for her. And I'm not invited along.

I find a creaky chair and a dark, quiet corner in the cloister. With my puffy and beanie on against the cold night air and by the light of my headlamp, I reread a portion of my great-aunt's journal. As I slip through those pages, an image of their lives, their past becomes clearer in my mind. It must have been so hard on them after their father left.

What could possibly cause a man to leave his home, his family, his country? The ugliness of war? Howard told me about his time in battle, but I still have a difficult time understanding why my great-grandfather did what he did. More difficult for his daughters, I'm sure. However, his pain was hell, was real. Something I can never imagine—a thing I wish the world was free of forever.

Where will my swollen feet take me in the next weeks? What will I find in a place called Astorga, at the address where Georgia's journal is being sent from, bit by bit?

Burgos, Spain
September 3, 1982
Patricia, if you ever come this way, you absolutely must visit the French Gothic cathedral in Burgos, the Cathedral of St. Mary. They started building it during the twelfth century. Writing this, my palms sweat when I try to grasp how long ago that was.

From Georgia's Travel Journal

TWENTY-THREE

Burgos, October 23, 2019

Before the city of Burgos, my path crosses under a busy freeway and into a park.

Groves of large trees absorb the whoosh of vehicles now behind me. Beth sent me a message saying there were options when entering Burgos. We chose the river path. I'm waiting for them here. I haven't seen Beth and Howard for a few days—or Macario.

I find a patch of green grass by the trail where I can wait for them, and lie against my backpack, a water bottle in one hand. Peacefulness wraps around me. I feel myself fade away.

That sweet, gorgeous Macario gently wakes me from a dream. A dream of him. His smile and perfect teeth, his dark curls draped around his handsome face. Wow, what a sight to wake up to! I tingle inside, in places that have never tingled in this way before.

Beth and Howard, and Cheryl and Yan—obviously a couple now—stand a few yards away. The look on their faces says they had half expected him to kiss me and wake me like I was Sleeping Beauty. Though I like him being here, being so close to me, the flush of red on my face shows my deeper feelings, both affection and worry.

I rise quickly, dust off loose pieces of dried grass and gather my things.

Together again, our group walks and talks about the things we have seen, thinking the end of another long trail day is close. However, the Camino says, *not so fast, you're going to enjoy this riverside park for a few miles first.* It goes by easily enough as we talk and laugh. Howard, always the one looking ahead, tells us we should visit the cathedral (*ugh, another one*) and about the openness of the *meseta*. He's talking to me more than the others because he knows I like big landscapes.

I have read about the meseta but Howard explains it so much better. We will trek this next section of the Camino Francés through the city of León and on to Astorga, through mostly wide-open countryside. We'll see nothing much more than wheat and barley fields for more than two hundred kilometers, Howard says. More than one hundred and twenty miles. I can't wait. Seriously, so much openness sounds amazing. He says we will pass through the city of León in the middle of those miles. And I know Astorga waits for me on the far edge of the meseta.

We all find bunks at the albergue close to the cathedral and go about our usual chores.

Now cleaned up and sipping soda at a café up the street from tonight's albergue, I wait again. Once everyone has cleaned up and put their laundry out to dry, we plan to tour the cathedral together. It stands right there in front of me, across the plaza from where I sit. Other pilgrims and many tourists wander past, all going to or returning from the stunning Cathedral of St Mary of Burgos.

I lean forward and duck my head under the umbrella above me to see the tops of the ornate, pale yellow fairytale towers. I've been reading some of the scanned pages of Georgia's journal now on my phone. She's telling her sister she needs to visit this place and how old it is. Words that never made their way to my grandmother.

Again, I question why she meant to send the journal and never did. Why was it only recently sent to us? Why, if Georgia wanted her sister to read these words, hadn't she sent the journal to Grandma Pat long before?

And who sends it now?

That last question—the one rattling in my head most often—makes me break out in beads of sweat on my forehead and under my arms. Who is it?

I look at the beautifully carved stone structure of the cathedral again. I've never felt as if I had Georgia's admiration for these old buildings. This one though, fantastic as it is, may change everything for me. A low sun lays golden shadows across the stone carvings and arches facing in my direction.

There's a chill in the air and I wonder if I should return to the albergue to get my jacket. Before I can decide, my Camino family strolls up the street coming my way. They are all smiles and laughter.

I turn back to the impressive view.

Beth comes up to my side. "What do you see?"

"A gothic façade." I say, looking back toward her.

"Is that so?" she says, a smile on her face, deepening the thin creases at her eyes and the corners of her mouth.

Once we're all together, Howard leads our mob around the cathedral to the entrance. We each pay the few euros to go inside.

Howard pays extra for the audio tour. He holds the device up to his ear and walks away from us, into the shadows.

I want to see how much I can remember from Father Ernesto's lessons at his cathedral in San Sebastián. The thought of his place, the kind priest, and my dead grandmother fill me with an anxious flight response. I want to run, to escape this beautiful space now falling in on me. I sit down for a minute, hopeful this feeling will pass quickly. Along the aisles I can see a dozen or more chapels, a suggestion of more in the transept arms and other parts of the building. The emotions slowly pass. I stand and restart my tour.

In a few minutes, Beth and Cheryl and I have come together. We walk in silence and in the same direction. We stop in front of one chapel or another, then move on. Beth stops to study a stone carving of an angel holding a human skull.

"Disturbing," she says.

I give a little nod in agreement. Chills cross over my shoulders, and I weave my arms together and over my chest. I should have gone back for my puffy. We continue our solemn stroll, sometimes crossing paths with Yan or Howard.

Whispered voices echo, causing ripples in the large, quiet space. High above, stained-glass windows let the low sun pour in to create contrasts of light and dark. We've come to the Tomb of El Cid; the main chapel is ahead of us.

We stand there quietly for a few moments, taking in the scene.

"It really is beautiful," says Cheryl. "Such artistry."

The religious figures and stories carved in stone and the many stained-glass windows are stunning. Carved and polished wooden benches line the walls leading to the altarpiece.

"It's overwhelming, really," says Beth.

The chill air still bites at my skin. "I'm going out to the

cloister yard to warm up," I tell them. Cheryl and Beth come with me.

Only slightly warmer outside the cathedral, we circle the stone fountain in the center of the yard and talk about what we see.

"You seem to know a lot about churches and such," says Beth to me.

"My Aunt Georgia, the one I told you about, she loved churches and cathedrals."

"Was she Catholic?" asks Cheryl.

I smile at the thought. "No. Not even religious. The opposite, I suppose. She was an adventurer."

"Have you learned these things from her journals?" asks Beth.

"Some, sure. A priest in San Sebastián and one in Pamplona proudly gave me tours of their cathedrals."

"Oh, how special," says Cheryl. Beth coos in agreement. We have finished our saunter through the cloister and walked through a door and entered another chapel.

"This is the chapel of Santiago," declares Beth. I look to her. She grins. "I'm cheating." She shows us a map of the cathedral on her phone.

Many of the images, statues, and carvings are becoming familiar to me. I know Santiago, St James, when I see him. I can tell you the difference between an apse and a transept, but not the difference between a cherub and an angel, or if there is one.

We quietly continue our tour. I bet we look like nuns seeking godliness in this holy place. My thoughts run quickly from a memory of my grandmother to the things Ernesto or Emil had taught me. I am warmed by these thoughts of those wonderful people. At least there are no carvings of human skulls in sight.

We split up. I move toward the shadows near the walls of the cathedral. I touch the cold porous stone. The wall draws energy from me. Not unkindly. My awareness combines with the building, like an antenna, which gives me a broader worldview. I hold the contact and close my eyes.

Easier now, I recall when Grandma Pat and I left the trail and found the Buen Pastor in San Sebastián. She was happy to follow in Georgia's footsteps, and not so happy for the noise of structural renovations when we arrived. As we entered the grand old building that day, I remember the look on her face, sort of like, *I'm here, Georgia.* I remember how tired she appeared as she started her tour. And how pale yet peaceful she looked when I last saw her lovely face.

These memories roll through and over me like ribbons of silk. Some feel yellow and worrisome, others red with fear, but so many more are shades of golden wheatstalks or lush green fields which make me feel better, warm inside. I've never had such feelings. What has my time at a church named Eunate done to me?

"You seem a million miles away," says Beth, the tone of her words tender.

"Yeah, I guess I was."

I realize Cheryl now stands on the other side of me. I look from Beth to Cheryl. "Georgia wanted my grandmother to come here, to visit this place, to walk the Camino," I say without thinking about it. I want it all to come out; I trust these women, perhaps even love them. But what would they think of me? I'm a liar. What might they think of me if they knew I virtually ran from my Aunt Tilly, and I'm only fifteen? *Not for long, girl.*

Before they can dig any deeper, Howard and Yan join us and say it's vino time. Beth and Cheryl agree.

I return with my jacket and find my friends at an open table large enough for all of us at a sidewalk café close to the albergue. More groups of pilgrims fill other tables. "Buen Camino" greetings ring out now and then. Cheryl and Yan have clicked together like magnet and iron, sitting very close. They hold hands. I note no one has said a thing about this . . . this promising romance.

Macario joins us. He had to call home. "My mama, she habla mucho. I could not leave her, leave the phone," he tells us as he sits down.

Howard pats him on the shoulder hard enough to almost spill the Spaniard out of his seat. "You're a good son."

We all laugh together.

They had ordered a bottle of red wine and a bottle of white wine. Glasses get filled. As usual, I put a hand over mine when one of the bottles comes my way. The waiter, an older man with a barrel chest, brings out the mineral water I ordered and happily fills my glass. I like his polite smile.

Still holding hands with Yan, Cheryl leans toward me. "So, you have your aunt's Camino diary. Do I understand correctly?"

"Yes. Well, it's my great-aunt's. My grandmother's sister. She walked the Camino in 1982."

"It must have been such a different journey then."

"I suppose. Less people, I'm sure."

"This idea pleases you, doesn't it?" she asks.

"It did. I'm getting used to it; happy I'm around people, with friends. The meseta, as Howard has described it, does sound fantastic, though," I say. She smiles.

"Your grandmother, did she walk the Camino?"

I set this up. Now I have to answer the question. But I'm still afraid it will all spill out of my mouth. A few more days and I don't think it will matter so much. Though, I cannot forget I have lied to them, and how much I hate this about me.

"She did. She walked part of the Camino del Norte." *Stick to the truth . . . with your lies.*

I see Beth across the table. She looks at me and smiles, before returning to her discussion with Howard.

If I'm to open my life to anyone, it's them, the first ones I told any of this story to.

Yan steals Cheryl's attention away.

After my birthday, day after tomorrow, I will say more. I'll also be honest with Macario.

Frómista, Spain
September 5, 1982
The hospitalera here remembers my father. She spent twenty minutes finding a yellowed registry and looking for Father's details. He was here in July 1977 and stayed on to help rebuild part of this albergue. Right here, yet I don't know how this makes me feel. Where is he now?

From Georgia's Travel Journal

TWENTY-FOUR

Frómista, October 25, 2019

Less than twenty miles today, and on my birthday. I'm sure Macario and the others are close behind. He likes talking with people. Beth calls him a "social butterfly," which is cute, like him.

I sent a message to the group on WhatsApp, letting them know that this albergue seems okay, just okay. It was my idea to stay here tonight because Georgia may have, and maybe her father before her. The others have now heard bits of their story. None of the real mysteries. I've told them about following in Georgia's footsteps and my interest in staying where she had. Nothing more.

I had been afraid to say much, to let them know my age. Now, though, I am sixteen. Does my truth matter anymore? Or have I been lying to myself, thinking my age would be a problem for them, when it's really something else? I try so hard to keep control, stay on my path. Yet, I know they can see me, my weaknesses, and my shyness. How I'm even aloof at times. I hate the word *aloof*.

This albergue, a private one, is an uninspired place—no Camino vibe. It's more of a hangout for the owner and his wife and their friends. Inside, a few of the bunks have been claimed, including mine. I sit in the courtyard, my bare feet resting on the clumped and scruffy-looking lawn, half listening to the conversations from the owner's group, picking out the Spanish words I recognize. They drink and gossip. I'm reading the journal again. I don't have the anatomy book with me, nor have I bothered to download an e-book, or—worse yet—have not started my own journaling practice. I could start today.

Every few days I tell Lou in texts to her about my time here, about the people I meet, my new friends, and about cute Macario. Those messages serve as my record for now. She tells me about her mother. Which is unbalanced in my favor. She's there, not me, and I feel sorry for Lou. She catches all her mother's grief and the anger meant for me for staying here in Spain.

Before checking into this albergue, I walked the few streets of the village and circled the eleventh-century Romanesque church three times. I wonder what it was like when my great-grandfather was here, so many years ago. Probably not much different from today. Fewer pilgrims, of course. I'm curious if this is where he stayed, where Georgia had spent a night or two. Did he spend time here in this courtyard? Did he plant this lawn? Did Georgia know these answers, and did she share them in her journal? Maybe he spent time thinking of what he had done, how he had left his family on their own. Did he think at all about the future? Could he? Howard said it's difficult getting beyond the darkness.

The owners of the place should take better care of the grass.

And what of my future? What will I do once I've returned home? What did my grandmother want of me?

Lou says Aunt Tilly has Grandma Pat's will. Says Tilly won't open it until I come home. She still can't stand the fact I have not returned home like a recalled diplomat. I feel blessed to have Lou buffering her mother's rants, keeping me from the worst of it. The time will come. But not now.

Lou wished me a happy birthday. Tilly probably doesn't remember its date, or care to.

The day has come and soon goes to the past, my past. Two hundred and fifty miles to Santiago still to go. And over two weeks to walk there. That is my priority. Well one of them, not the highest.

I open my Camino Francés app and look ahead at the villages, towns, and cities before Astorga.

For the tenth time, I punch the Astorga address into a map app, look at the satellite view of the home, wondering what I'll find there, and who. The secret sender. Returning to the Camino app, I calculate five or six more stages before I arrive in the city. Again, my heart pounds at the thought of it. One hundred miles, less than a week from now. So close.

I expect the others, my Camino Francés family, will arrive soon. It's time I took a shower.

Before I get fully dressed, they arrive, Macario in the lead. He looks so strong, so happy. I raise my arms and pull on the long-sleeved shirt I wear during cool evenings. The weather turns now and then, a forecast of things to come.

The group has grown by a few more pilgrims. One guy with long light-brown dreadlocks has a small acoustic guitar strapped to his backpack. I hope he plays it for us tonight. There's a teeny woman beside him. And an older woman who has the same blue backpack as mine, same brand, just as new.

There's a shuffle of bunk selections, greetings, and introductions. Not so concerned and modest as in the early days of my journey, I slowly finish dressing. My wet hair is a tangled mess, tendrils hanging in my eyes. Before dealing with my hair, I need to hang out clothes to dry.

An assortment of wine and beer bottles line the wall like they are up for inspection; the group had stopped at the supermarket by the church, someone says.

Macario has picked a top bunk not far from mine. Heading to the showers, he stops at my bunk.

"Not too hot today. Did you enjoy?" he asks, as cheerful as always.

"Yes, it was marvelous." *Was marvelous?* He still ties my tongue. "The miles seemed to fly by today. I sort of got in this zone, you know?"

He nods his head. "Is the beauty of the Camino, no?"

"Sí." I look to the clothes and soap in his grasp. "Time for a shower? It felt good, but you might want to get there before the hot water runs out," I say with a smile. I look into his eyes. I have never met anyone like this Spaniard. He is so beautiful. Okay, so, handsome. A heat rises from my middle, blankets my neck, then I feel the warmth of it on my face.

He reaches up with one hand and swipes aside a strand of damp hairs, tucking them behind my ear. "I see you after my shower. Beth has planned an evening of fun for all of us."

He is sweet. My knees go weak. He turns and walks toward the showers. I watch him go, the bundle of wet clothes still in my hands, beads of sweat on my lip.

I like him, the idea of being with him. I have no experience with romance. Any romantic involvement with him gets complicated, a mistake. I'm still young; he's still too old—if I'm to listen to my grandmother. So much of my energy goes to acting as if I am eighteen and maintaining some sort of protective wall. What does Macario think of me, want from me?

So complicated. *Well, whose fault is that?*

I'm about to go and hang out my clothes when Cheryl and Beth stop by.

"Our host said we can use the table in the front patio this evening. We're going to have a little party," says Cheryl as she nods her head in the direction of their collection of bottles.

"We'll see what we can order up for food, too, of course," says Beth as she glances to my stomach. She looks like she expects my abdomen to growl on command. They smile at her joke. I display a tight grin. It would be a shame if I leave Spain with such an odd reputation.

It's getting late. Everyone has showered. Beers get passed down the table. I sip from my water bottle. Beth and I have organized take-out from a restaurant down the street. An order sheet and menu make the rounds. Yan and Macario will return to the restaurant and pick up our meals when the restaurant calls back.

The sun has set, and the temperature drops fast. Phil, the guy with the dreads, tunes his guitar. He called it a parlor guitar. It's smaller than my father's, which I haven't seen in years. Macario and the little woman, Celeste, chat about a place along today's route where they got water from a two-thousand-year-old Roman well. Yan brings the order sheet to Beth. She's going to run it over to the restaurant.

I'm at a corner seat where I can take in the scene. Yan hesitantly offers me a beer. I politely decline. Phil begins to play. I'm quite happy right here like this. Other pilgrims, some in their own Camino collectives, come and go. Every time, someone shouts "Buen Camino" or "Ultreia," another pilgrim greeting, we happily reply with the same.

Before I know it, our meals have come, been gobbled up, and the mess erased from the table. I got chilled and while I went for my puffy jacket more wine bottles have arrived. I retake my perch at the end of the table. Macario, across from me, talks with Yan.

Yan, the Swedish guy, doesn't speak any Spanish, and only a little English, but they manage.

"Can I sit with you?" asks the older woman. "I'm Deanna by the way."

"Yes, of course," I reply, and scoot my butt over a bit.

"Beth tells me you are from California. Is that right?" she asks.

"Yes, not far from San Diego. And you?" I think she's from the US, but I hear the hint of an accent in her words.

"I'm from Ontario, Canada. It's my Dutch and French Canadian heritage you hear in the way I speak."

Another mind reader. Or am I so easy to read?

Phil begins to play a song I know. I perk up. It's an old one, a song Adam used to play at gatherings in the camp where I grew up.

"You know this one?" asks Deanna.

"Yes. Adam, my father, he used to play this when I was little." I sit forward and clasp my hands in front of me on the table. Phil plays well, and his guitar sounds amazing for being carried around on his back in the sunlight all day.

Deanna leaves me alone while I listen to Phil play. She pours some more wine into her glass, passes the bottle on to Macario and Yan, then holds her glass in her lap, listening to the music. I close my eyes.

When Phil finishes the song, he declares a need to pee, and he'll come back soon. I wake from the dream world I floated in—lying in a hammock between two cedar trees, breathing in the scent of evergreens, and listening to my father play the same song.

"Welcome back," says Deanna. Macario smiles at me.

"Yeah, sorry. I was back there with my parents," I admit.

"Can you tell us about them?" Deanna says. Macario and Yan agree with her, nodding in unison.

"Can I have a little wine?" I ask Yan.

Someone finds a glass and Yan fills it to where I point with my fingertip. This is a delaying tactic. A fact Deanna seems aware of, but waits patiently.

With the wine glass in my hands, I begin. "Adam grew marijuana at a commune in the Pacific Northwest." I say this, and then let it sink in. They wait politely. Phil has returned and starts to pluck his guitar strings again. Hushed conversations down the table linger and weave with the music. "We lived in an old wooden shack built for scouts and their leaders during summer outings. Winters were brutal cold there. We burned a lot of firewood during those long months."

I'm not looking at my friends, not sipping from the wine glass. I'm a kid again, living in a forest with a bunch of crazy people. "A dozen or so couples lived there, all of them sort of loony or strung out or drunk all the time."

Deanna puts a warm hand on my forearm. I look into her eyes, and then to the two guys. Beth now stands at the end of the table beside me. I look up and into her eyes.

"You must miss them, your parents," declares Beth. I nod and my head droops. I don't want her to see my shame. I love these people, but I've lied to them.

Tears well up. I want to tell them the whole truth. I could tell them about my grandmother. Though I would start bawling. I shake off the feeling, focus on my bare feet on the cool patio stones, grounding myself. The wine warming in my grip finds its way to my lips. I let a large swallow of the smooth liquid slip down my throat and enjoy the acidic afterglow as it bites at my tongue.

After pulling in a deep breath I begin, "My grandmother, Grandma Pat, she saved me from that place. She took me to live with her in California. We live in a small town in the mountains. She has a café. She's famous for her apple pies." I say these words as I see myself there before we had left for Spain. It's easier in a way; like acting, it's a good way to tell a lie.

Phil has stopped playing again. Everyone looks to our end of the table, at me. It's as if they know my truth.

Phil puts his guitar aside. The wine is nearly gone, and Howard begins to talk. He raises the subject of tomorrow's destination, how far of a walk it is to this village or that town. Thank you, Howie.

Beth chimes in from where she stands over our end of the table. "Howie says our walk to the city of León will take four days. He and I will take a rest day there. We want to visit the cathedral and a museum and a palace."

A few in our group see the value of this idea. I worry I'd deliberately delay my arrival in Astorga. Conversations spring up at each corner of the patio, some people now standing, others still sitting. I, of course, wish to walk alone again, see where the day takes me. For three days now, we have been on the meseta. There is little to nothing out there, almost no shade, endless tilled fields, and bright sunshine. It's beautiful to me.

We have one more week of what Cheryl calls "The Grand Exposure" until Astorga. From there, my grandmother's guidebook says the Camino enters the mountains and eventually Galicia, where Santiago and our destination waits for us.

A few in the group consider the larger town of Carrión de los Condes for tomorrow night's stay. I think of one of the smaller villages several miles farther on.

Macario walks with me to the dorm room. He kisses me on the cheek and says a sweet good night.

A tingle again blazes inside of me; this has been the best birthday ever, ignoring the glaring fact I feel bad for being a cowardly liar.

Carrión de los Condes, Spain
September 6, 1982

I've lost him, my wayward father. I had a lead. A man who worked with him in Frómista told me Father left there, returning to the Camino, but planned to find work in Carrión de los Condes. I have asked many of the locals now I am here. None of them remember him. I have been distracted though: I met a gorgeous fellow, my age, a shopkeeper's son. I think I'll stay another day.

From Georgia's Travel Journal

TWENTY-FIVE

Carrión de los Condes, October 26, 2019

A cool wind blows a swell of dust and leaves along a side street. I can hear it coming, see it reaching above nearby buildings. It bursts across the intersection I walk through.

Old men seated on a park bench calmly ease a shoulder to the wind and duck their heads away, hold their caps down. I stop, turn my back to it, and close my eyes. I'm at the western edge of the town. Some of my friends will stay here tonight. Still early in the day, I've refilled my water bottles for a long dry stretch ahead and will continue to Caladilla de la Cueza, ten miles farther along the Camino.

The dust and leaves pass us by, and the wind tames. It has been gusty since mid-morning. Nowhere to hide from its offenses out on the expansive plains of the meseta, something has blown into my shoe. Concentrating on walking straight and upright to regular wind gusts, I didn't notice the blister on my right heel. Now it has erupted. I stop and sit on a vacant bench and tend to the frayed skin. The hole is as big as a quarter and nearly deep enough to expose the subcutaneous tissue below the dermis layer. I go to work.

My foot tended to and feeling much better, I start walking again. After crossing the Carrión River, and walking beyond the outskirts of the town, I see more open landscape ahead. The Camino, now following a farm road, stretches off straight as an arrow into the distance. There are no other pilgrims ahead of me.

I look back. I see someone with a backpack walking powerfully in my direction. I slow my pace to see if it's someone I know or have met before, however briefly. This person is dressed differently from most pilgrims—a new someone then. She wears desert camouflage pants and carries a tan, military-style backpack. I see a glow of rippling energy around her, a soft yellow, edged in red. Curious.

She quickly catches me. A short ponytail of light brown hair, pulled so tight from her head it points straight back, droops like a rooster tail. Above, another camo pattern, a faded wide-brimmed hat.

My heart rate rises. My mind wants to duck away from this person. But something deep inside says, *talk to her.* "Buen Camino."

"You too," says the woman. She is much taller than me, has thick, powerful legs, and might outweigh me by half.

I match her speedy stride. "Are you a pilgrim?" I ask tentatively. Her size and serious face makes me nervous, but her energy lures me in.

"Yeah, that's what they tell me."

"Are you stopping in Caladilla de la Cueza tonight?"

She looks over to me with a dark stare.

"Yeah, Cal-a-dil-la, that's it. Where I'll meet the boys," she says with an ugly, down-beat finish to her sentence.

"Me too. My name is Summer." The sentence takes all I have. I slow down, expecting her to continue without another word. She slows too.

I draw in a gulp of air. "These last miles seem a marathon in this wind. I'm from California, by the way," I say, ending with a quizzical tone.

"Name's Sara, no h." Her hard-edged voice comes out gruff and has an accent. "I'm from the UK. Originally from a town near London. Now I call the town of Chipping Norton home base."

I don't immediately come up with another question to ask. A gust nearly knocks me over, pushing me toward Sara. An intuitive trekking pole steadies me, and I move back to my side of the lane. I don't think the wind fazes her at all. I spit some grit from between my teeth and cough up something from deep in my throat.

"It's good for you," Sara says.

"The dirt in my mouth?"

"That too, I suppose," she says. "But no, I meant making an effort, battling a foe, learning to work toward what you want, and things get difficult sometimes."

"My Grandma Pat said stuff like that."

"Smart lady."

We walk on in silence for a long while. Sara won't make it easy, but I like her for some reason.

"Going to stop," she says, and she does. I do too, a few feet away. She pulls a hose from under a hook and loop patch on her chest and sucks water in for a long time. I pull a bottle from its pouch and drink as well.

"You said you would meet other people in Caladilla?"

"Yeah, the boys. That's what I call them. Bunch of pricks, if you ask me. We're on mission here. Sort of. We're all veterans; seen some shit. They say walking this trail—if you can call it a trail—will help us work things out." She looks around for a moment, then looks up the path ahead of us. "Been out here for three days now. Lots of nothing if you ask me. Even the farm boys are scarce."

"Did you start in Burgos?" I ask as we resume our walk.

"Yes, Burgos. I kind of liked it. Big though," she says. "You've got a limp in your step, little girl."

Little girl? Maybe I won't like her. "Yeah. A blister. I took care of it back there. Part of the suffering, right?"

"I don't have a single one," Sara says proudly.

"None?"

"Not one. But yeah. Crap comes your way, you survive it, or you don't."

She's back to her normal pace. I try to keep up but eventually have to slow down. Sara slows again, matching my pace. I glance at her pants.

"Yeah, odd, huh?" I don't respond. "I didn't have the money to buy all the fancy stuff on their list. So, I'm wearing what I had, and what I'm most comfortable in."

"Are you in the military?"

"Was once. Signed up a decade ago. Saw conflict later but can't say where. Because we were never there."

I crane my neck to read her expression. She's upset, eyes squinted.

She looks down, inspecting the farm road, then over to me. "Those lies they tell, that's why I resigned."

I sense the finality of this direction in our conversation. "Will you walk to Santiago?"

"That's the mission," she says. "Bet the boys are soaking in beer by now. Could use one myself."

A dust devil rises out of the dry soil a hundred yards away. In a moment, it finds us. All this openness and it homes right in on the two of us. Without thinking about it, I duck in behind Sara. When the dust settles and I reappear, she inclines her face to me again, a smile forming under the shade of her hat. It is nearly threadbare and flops in the wind, but she has it secured, a thin strap tight under her chin.

By late afternoon, we see Caladilla de la Cueza, a speck of a village on the grand expanse. The road we have walked forever delivers us right to the municipal albergue at the edge of the village. Sara says the boys will be there. Or the nearest bar.

"There is a private albergue next door. I plan to stay there," I tell her.

"Think they have room for another body?" asks Sara.

"Easy enough to find out. Don't you need to stay with your group?"

"Some things are not worth the struggle, little girl."

Oh, I'm going to kick her. Then run like hell. "Let's go see if they have enough bunks."

We're about to turn the corner when several men spill out of the door at the muni, fifty feet away. They see Sara and call out something indistinguishable. She ignores them. They howl at her again and head for a bar across the street.

"Let's go," she says, then powers to our left.

I hurry to follow her as we cross a patch of dirt in front of the Albergue Camino Real. It looks smaller than the muni next door and has a soda machine by the entrance.

"If this place has room for me, I'll go tell the lieutenant where I'm staying tonight. He'll get upset. But tough you-know-what."

In routine fashion, we have our credentials stamped and are assigned bunks. We have two of four bunks in a room at the end of the hall. Sara does a very thorough inspection for bedbugs and any other issues before she allows me to step inside the room. "Recon," she calls it.

We find the showers, wash out a few things, and sit down to watch our clothes flop and twist on the line in the courtyard. A gorgeous green lawn surrounds an inviting swimming pool. It's too cold for swimming, and the wind still whistles through the town, but it makes a pretty scene. Dust occasionally blasts into the courtyard and settles on us and the few other pilgrims hanging out or lying on the lawn. There's an old man close by, a sour look on his long, boney face. He sits alone at one of the tables, a worn, leather-bound book in front of him.

"From California, eh?" says Sara, a light tone in her voice.

"So-Cal, they call it. I'm from a place in the mountains not far from the city of San Diego."

"I like small towns," she says. "Don't much like people, all the noise they cause. I could settle down right here, happy as a lark."

"I know what you mean."

Sara sits forward and twists her chair in my direction, its metal feet scraping on the rough concrete finish, sounding like a rusty chunk of iron being dragged over a granite block. She winces, eyes pinched tight. It's a long while before she opens them again. She says, "I don't know what it is about you, little girl, but you're easy to talk with. What have you done to me, surfer girl?"

"I don't surf, never have. Only been to the beach a few times. And the name's Summer."

She grimaces again. "Sorry. I think what I say is funny. Never comes out right," she says. Her eyes are on me now. "When do we go get something to eat?"

"It's probably late enough, now. They'll have a pilgrim's menu at the bar. The one across the street," I say.

"Think there's another place in town?"

I understand her meaning and do a quick search with my phone. "Yeah. There's one a couple of blocks west."

The old man has been eyeing us, an angry look on his face. Sara has noticed him too.

I check the phone again for directions to the restaurant.

"The Camino's no place for those damn smart-assed-phones," declares the old man. His accent sounds eastern-European. Me, the expert now. He's old. Like my great-grandfather if he's alive, and scrawny, bones showing through thin, veined skin.

"That right, old man?" says Sara as she stands and steps toward him. Her height towers and then arches over him.

The anger doesn't leave his face, he doesn't say another word, but doesn't back down from the huge army veteran either.

I get up. "Let's go, Sara. It's only a five-minute walk from here to the restaurant," I say as I reach out to touch her arm. I think better of it a millisecond before she snap-turns to me. She slowly straightens. A rage inside fades and she finally grins at me.

Another village on the plains of Spain
September 8, 1982
I invited myself to sit with some old men playing cards, a game they call "Mus." There were four of them. I pulled a chair up to a corner and, without giving them a chance to chase me away, asked my questions. They made it clear they did not like a woman at their table. Once I asked about a man, an American man who may have worked in the village, they came to life. Every man in the game remembered my father.

From Georgia's Travel Journal

TWENTY-SIX

Caladilla de la Cueza, October 26, 2019

At dinner, Sara orders a thin pork steak, broad bean soup and more warm bread. I order the mixed salad and tonight's pasta dish. We both ask for the custard dish for dessert. As we eat, the patio fills with loud, clamoring pilgrims. The fragrances of fried meats and warm bread and wine take over. I don't feel my normal urge to run.

Our plates now empty, Sara says, "I love the food here, little — I mean, Summer. 'Good grub' the Yanks would call it."

"The Yanks?" I ask.

"Yeah, you Americans," she says with a smile. "The Aussies call it 'tucker.'" She picks up her beer and sits back in her seat, looking at me with an appraising, sideways glance. "So, you appear awful young. What are *you* doing out here? I imagine other people have asked you this question. You'll have a good answer by now."

Unexpectedly, this moment feels like puzzle pieces fitting perfectly together. My mind rolls back to the beginning and the weeks of walking to here, this place in the middle of nowhere, sitting with a British army veteran. I look around the patio. The other pilgrims around us still eat and drink, talk and laugh. The shiny aluminum chairs and tables with various types of people from all over the world are now such familiar sights it all feels almost homelike. The wind has gone away, and the temperature again falls fast. Thankfully, I brought my jacket. Sara doesn't seem to notice the cold.

What I don't understand is why this woman is so easy to talk with.

"I'm looking for my great-grandfather." I met Sara only this afternoon and here I am telling her this part of my story. She has turned her head and now has her dark eyes locked on me. "He was a veteran, too. Fought in a war a long way from home. He came here to get away from what, I couldn't possibly imagine. The pain. The suffering. The memories."

Sara's gaze softens; she lowers her face. "All of those things."

I wait for her to explain if she can.

"Mine is a military family. Damn near every one of us has had something to do with the British army. Have a cousin who went into the Royal Marines. At family gatherings he gets pummeled with a load of shit, but he always wears his dress blues when we get together. A stubborn lot, we are." She sits forward and wraps her big hands around the beer mug, interlacing her fingers. "Not going into the military wasn't really an option for me. My parents were proud of me the day I signed up. And very disappointed when I left that life, resigned. I told them how it was different from their time in the service of king and country. The waste of money, time, people's lives. And the ridiculous lies told to justify it all. God, I hated it. They listened, my parents did, but haven't had much to say to me since then."

I thought it was bad living with a bunch of stoners. The commune was a piece of cake compared to Sara's life. "My great-grandfather got drafted. My grandmother told me her father had no choice."

Sara sits quietly, slumped shoulders and a downcast face, like this is all she has left in her this evening. I finish my soda. The café owner collects our plates. Sara orders another beer.

The beer arrives. Sara perks up, takes a long pull from the mug, and sets it down. "The guys I'm with . . . supposed to be with, they understand. They try to hide it, roughhousing, joking all the time. The lieutenant and the counselor who runs this program we're in let them go at it, saying it's part of the process. We—each of us in some way—saw things in battle no one should ever have to see. The counselor says we will go through phases of release as we walk the Camino. I'm not so sure. I keep waiting."

"He could have been on to something, then. My great-grandfather, I mean. Did he go through phases of recovery while walking through here all those years ago?"

"You said you hunt for him." This isn't a question, but it is. Georgia's journal sent me looking for him. But I only have part of her story, their story. When will the rest arrive so Lou can forward it to me?

I know Sara wants more. There is more, even without the ending. "It's so hard to talk—"

Sara sits straight up. Her eyes dart to a place right above me. I turn sharply and look up. He smiles down on me.

"Macario!" Beside him stands Phil, guitar slung across his shoulders.

"You know these guys?" asks Sara, a guarded tone in her voice.

"Oh, yeah. Sara, this is Macario and Phil," I say as I point to each of them. "Sit with us, guys."

Sara slides her chair closer to me. The guys take seats across the table from us, and the cute Spaniard waves our waiter over.

"Did you just get here?" I ask Macario.

"Sí. We walk long day to catch up to you," he says with a grin.

Phil leans his guitar against the side of the building. "We're damn thirsty, sista."

They order beers and select meals from the day's menu. Sara stays quiet. And Macario hasn't taken his eyes off me for more than a moment. He leans across the table, puts his hands out in front of me, and ignores Sara.

I feel her body heat. She's protective of me. This feels sort of weird, but not weird. It's like we've known each other forever.

"Sara, I met Macario after Pamplona. He's part of my Camino family. And Phil too. He plays his guitar and sings better than anyone I know. Except for my father, of course."

A young girl in pink tights brings out the beers for the guys.

Sara looks toward me and nods. I see an understanding there. Somehow, we communicate without words. She drains the last of her beer and sits forward. "I had better go talk with the lieutenant and the counselor. Smooth those feathers, right?" She pushes her chair back and stands. "I will see you later, at the barracks."

I glance up. "Yeah, sounds good. See you in a little while." She's not looking at me but boring a glare into Macario, his gaze locked on me. Phil takes in the whole scene, as if he's a movie camera recording a documentary film on Camino romances. Macario still ignores Sara. She grunts and leaves.

I hang out with the guys. With all the willpower I can summon, I don't take Macario's hands. Thankfully, their meals come soon. I relax. They plow through their food like they haven't eaten in a week, which makes me smile at them both.

Minutes later, and plates clean, some women Phil had met days earlier ask him to play his guitar for them. He is happy to oblige and moves to the far end of the patio.

For a while we listen to Phil play and the women clap and ask him for more. But the whole time I'm thinking about how I have told someone I just met about why I am here in Spain. Not everything, but this still surprises me. It also—sitting here with Macario so close—becomes clearer that he should know my truth.

"Walk me back to my albergue?"

Without a word, he smiles a broad, toothy, beautiful smile, and gets up. He takes my hand and helps me up. In a smooth move he tucks my arm under his and leads me down the street. On our left, buildings of the village, on our right, the meseta. Now we are away from the lights of the restaurant, and we can see the stars sparkling in the night sky. A cold breeze comes up the street and into our faces. But he smiles.

"I need to tell you something."

"Sí. What is it, my Summer girl?" he says, controlling a laugh. "I practice saying this." His smile broadens.

Damn. "I'm not eighteen like I led you and our friends to believe." I have ripped the tape right of the blister. And it hurts. He has let my arm go but holds onto my hand. We walk under a streetlight and stop. I look into his eyes. He's not sure what I have said to him. "I turned sixteen and few days ago."

He drops my hand. I think he's mad. My muscles tense even more. My shoulders would draw right up to my ears if I let them.

"This . . . this surprise me. Yes."

"I'm so sorry. I like you, like being with you. And I'm sorry I have led you on."

"It is best to know now. I like you too, Summer. I like you

very much. But is not right. Not right the way I feel." He inspects the ground for a moment, steps back a half step more.

"I'm so—"

"No, no. Is okay," he says, interrupting me. "I was not honest too. I thought you did not like me, could not like me. And I have lied too." He looks up.

"I do like you, a lot, Macario." I even like saying his name. It's as gorgeous and smooth sounding as he is handsome. "But if I were with you like we both might want—" *Wait. He lied to me.* I freeze.

"I never told you my age, which was like lying to you. I am twenty-four years old. I have finished college. I go to new job after we finish our walk into Santiago."

"Whoa, I didn't expect . . ."

"But you do like me?" he asks.

"Yes, of course. How could I not like you? Are we friends?"

"Yes, yes. Always friends. Siempre amigos, siempre."

We finish our walk to the albergue. He and Phil stay here too. We had never asked. And the guys will sleep in our room. They got the last two bunks—across from Sara's and mine. As we discover this, Sara tromps down the hall and enters the room. Seconds later, Phil comes in.

No one says a word. Until I burst out laughing. Macario and Phil join in. Sara looks stern for a moment, then joins in the hilarity. Someone in the next room pounds a fist on the thin wall, immediately getting our attention.

We finally settle down and climb into our sleeping bags. The light in the hall is turned off, but there is light coming from outside, giving a slightly orange glow to our tiny space.

Macario is across from me. We are in the top bunks. He stretches out a hand toward me. I reach toward him with mine. Our hands don't quite touch. He smiles and says, "Amigos."

"Siempre."

I lie back, the past day flowing through my mind.

"Summer?" says Sara.

"Yeah."

"I have to walk with the boys tomorrow."

"Oh. Okay. Sorry." And I am sorry. We just met today but I feel a connection with Sara. Different from the friendships I've made with others on the Camino, but just as close.

Reliegos, Spain
September 12, 1982
The clues the men in the Mus game gave me about Father lead to nothing. His trail has gone cold. The closer I sometimes think I get to Father the farther away he feels. Time has erased his handsome face from my memory. But the feeling of how sad he always seemed will never fade. Is it truly even possible to find him? I am certain Patricia now considers this a silly notion. Maybe it is.

From Georgia's Travel Journal

TWENTY-SEVEN

León, October 29, 2019

León is a small city in comparison to many, but it's huge and busy and overwhelming when walking in from the meseta. As the distances have worked out, I will stay here tonight. I also want to stop at an ATM. I have plenty of euros, but looking ahead, this seems like a good place to pick up more cash. Not many businesses in the villages and towns we pass through accept debit or credit cards.

Last night, during dinner with my friends, Beth told me where they planned to stay for two nights in León. I reserved a room for tonight at the same place. It's not far from the cathedral.

It's a nice hotel, nothing too fancy. There's a café next door with the usual outside tables and chairs. I'm waiting there for the others to arrive. I took a wonderful, lengthy shower and washed out a few things in the sink. But now I'm sipping on a cola and watching people come and go. Later, I will take the short walk to the plaza and the cathedral.

"Are you walking the Camino?" asks a woman at a table beside me, Australian accent, I think. I slide around in my seat. The gray-haired woman is older than my grandmother was when she died. A man of about the same age sits next to her, a digital SLR camera in his hands. He looks like he's checking out pictures taken today.

"Yes," I respond. "And you?"

"Oh, yes," she says. "This is our tenth Camino. Not always the Camino Francés, mind you."

I understand the concept, now. "The Camino got into your blood, eh?"

"Yes, indeed," the man says, still not looking up from his camera.

"After we retired," says the woman. "We're from Melbourne, Australia, you see. When we left our jobs, we decided the Camino would be our first big adventure. We've been coming back every year since."

I scoot my chair around so I'm not craning my neck to chat with them. We talk about the various Caminos in Europe, about the people you meet, about the plains of Spain, and then discover our common interest in churches and cathedrals. Without going into much detail, I tell the couple of my great-aunt and her love for the cathedrals, how she wrote about them in her journal. We agree the cathedrals in Burgos and Santo Domingo de la Calzada have been our favorites.

"And then there's the grand old cathedral in Santiago, our destination," says the man. His name is Justin. Hers is Cecilia. He tells me a little of that cathedral's history, what to expect, and the things to look for when I arrive. In a few minutes we determine I will arrive in Santiago a week before them. They are in no hurry. Why am I in such a hurry? I have a mystery to solve and need to be at the airport in Santiago on the tenth of next month. November closes in. So does Astorga. I will be there on the first of the month. There, I'll find what I can. And then the real work begins. "First we must scale those mountains and enter Galicia before we can think about Santiago," says Justin.

Cecilia grumbles at the thought of it.

"I haven't looked beyond Astorga," I say. "I know we will come to the mountains and the climbing starts after that city. But looking so far ahead has not been a priority."

"There's weather to contend with too," says Cecilia. As soon as the words come out of her mouth, a twist of wind and fine dust rounds the corner a block away and works its way down the street toward us. Justin and Cecilia instinctually cover their drinks with one hand. My soda is gone so I don't worry about it. I close my eyes and wait until the twister passes. "We may even have a fair bit of rain tomorrow."

The weather has been decent most days. I hadn't been watching the forecasts. Cecilia and I look to our smartphones and the weather report. I had better dig out my rain gear. It's been in the bottom of my pack since Pamplona.

From behind, I hear Howard's familiar voice and Beth's arms wrap around me. "It's so good to see you," she says. When I look up, Howard stands at her side.

I introduce them to Justin and Cecilia. Before they check in to the hotel, we make plans to meet at the cathedral and later get together for dinner at one of the restaurants on the plaza. Beth remembers one she especially liked from their previous Camino. Justin and Cecilia will meet friends they want me to meet. Younger people, closer to my age, Justin tells me, a hint of curiosity in his words. I don't say a thing. Let them think what they will. Beth grins at me.

And it's settled, we will all meet for dinner at Beth's suggested restaurant.

After our tour and dinner, we tired pilgrims return to our rooms. I want to get up early.

It is still dark out when I hit the streets the next morning. And sure enough, there is a mist of cool moisture falling from the sky. I zip up my raincoat and buckle my backpack straps. The pack has a rainproof cover pulled over it. I hope the best for my things inside the pack.

Streetlights glow their familiar orange and illuminate the rain drops, which fall larger by the minute. At the corner, I enter the huge square where I had such a great time with my friends last night. The space opens before me, the lighted face of the cathedral looming beautifully over the scene. Its gothic presence reaching up, the tips of its spires lost in the storm clouds.

Last night I saw an ATM at a nearby corner. I find it again and look around. There isn't a soul in sight. I kind of wish Sara stood here, watching my back. I've never had any problems, but Father Ernesto's warning is always there. Where is my British friend, anyway?

I hear water dripping from downspouts and the rumble of a truck in the distance. The cash machine waits for me, lighted and familiar, and one from the bank I've used most often to retrieve more euros from my grandmother's account. It doesn't feel odd taking her money. I know she wants me to, and to finish our project, our quest.

I slip her debit card into the slot and wait for the machine to respond. I don't bother to select the English version. This is an easy process now. It welcomes me and asks for the PIN. I enter the numbers and wait again. A command comes up asking what I want to do. I select the option to withdraw cash. Grandma Pat's bank has a daily limit in dollars, and I make sure I'm asking for an amount below it in euros.

The screen changes again. I wait for the sound of money being counted out and delivered to the slot below. Nothing happens for a moment. Then a new screen comes up. It's difficult to translate words I've not seen before. They don't look good. Near as I can tell, there's a problem with the card. The session gets canceled automatically.

I try again, this time going with the English version. Same result. And now I can read it, too precisely. The card or the PIN were not approved. *Crap.*

Now what do I do? I have taken this process for granted. This card *did* work.

I try once more. Again, not approved.

I step back from the machine and into the rain, which has doubled or tripled. I move closer to the building and pull off my pack. After layer upon layer of protection, I find my grandmother's wallet and extract another card, another one my grandmother had put a travel advisory on, telling her bank about going to Spain. Hope returns.

Quick as possible, I go through the process—using the English instructions—and wait.

Again, no sounds of cash being counted, and then the dreaded message. Not approved.

Tilly. *Damn you.*

I know she did this. I paw through the wallet again and find another card. I don't allow my hopes to go anywhere this time. The buttons are now wet and slippery from my previous attempts. Probably from tears I'm not aware of too. Same miserable result. For the longest time, I stand there, stunned, unable to think. Finally, I put everything away and close my pack and pull the rain cover over it again.

It's all over; I'm done. Tilly will finally have me doing things her way. I'll bet she's kicking herself for not thinking of this long before now. My hopes of reaching Santiago are dead. I still have some cash. At least I can make it to Astorga.

I slip my pack back onto my shoulders. Everything about me is numb. I click the buckles together.

I take a step. This usually helps. I'll walk for a while. I take another step and—

Darkness. I'm flat on my back. My eyes open to raindrops. They slam shut. There's a booming voice in the rain, very close. My eyes fly open. I blink raindrops from them. I'm lying on the plaza stones, rain pouring down on me. There's this huge man standing over me, looking like a raging bull. He's yelling at me in Spanish, hands flying around and pointing this way and that. I catch a few curse words and the Spanish word for death or dead, *muerte*.

Like a turtle flailing about and nearly helpless, I finally dig a fingertip or two into a seam in the stones and roll off my backpack and onto my side. There's a delivery truck idling close to us. Did it hit me? Did he run me over? I reach for my legs.

He's still ranting and raving while he helps me to my feet. He calms down a little and asks, "Estás bien?" He's looking me over and wiping loose bits from my clothes and backpack.

I step back. Water streams from my face and hands. From everywhere now.

Like Aunt Tilly attacking me from afar wasn't bad enough, I've been hit by a truck. I assure the man I'm okay and do my best to tell him I will be more careful. He goes back to his truck and climbs into the cab, grumbling to himself the whole time. The truck roars away and across the huge square.

I'm awake now, for certain. Dawn has broken and filtered daylight paints the city. The sky falls in waves now. Streetlights wink out as I find bronze scallop shells of the Camino de Santiago in the sidewalks and alleys showing me the way out of León. I put a hand in my pocket and finger the few euro bills and coins I have in there. Then I place a palm over the money belt Grandma Pat bought for me and I try to intuit how much money I have left in there. I'd guess there's three-hundred euros in the money belt and twenty or thirty more in my pocket.

I start doing math problems in my head, not my favorite pastime. I prefer memorizing anatomical terms and associations to anything mathematics related. The human body makes so much more sense to me. So far, I've probably been spending more than forty euros a day on average. I'd need four or five hundred euros to make it all the way to Santiago.

What can I do to make this work? What can I do to ruin Tilly's sneaky move to force me to return to California? What can I do to make certain I don't fail? I can figure this out as I walk in the pouring rain.

The sky is a lighter gray when I return to the present moment. I've never seen so much mud, never walked for hour after hour in a downpour. In the forest, where Adam and Laura live, the sky knew how to rain, come down hard. But there I could duck under a huge cedar tree to wait out a deluge or go back to our cabin and throw more logs on the fire.

To make things worse, I've taken the *scenic route*. The Camino app had two routes to the village of Hospital de Orbigo. Thinking I needed time away from people, to struggle with my math problems, and curse Tilly, I've strayed from the more direct route along a highway. Big mistake. There isn't a soul out here, not even a farm tractor or a scruffy old dog.

My shoes weigh a ton, mud sticks to them in thick layers. My feet are soaked to the bone. And my legs are now coated with mud dripping from knee to ankle, adding to the mess on my mushy shoes.

From the side of the farm road, I stop and look around. I haven't seen a thing but rain and mud in hours. I drift to the center of the road trying to avoid huge clumps of mud left by a tractor an hour or, perhaps, days ago. My trekking poles sometimes slip sideways. I've nearly face planted or fallen on my ass again a dozen times by now.

The rainfall doubles again. It's raining so hard I can't see more than a quarter mile. Not that there's anything interesting out here to see anyway. I'd love to see a church steeple peeping up from the next village, a hint of a place to dry off and warm up for a while.

I go on. Still nothing but more mud and a straight path. There isn't so much as a bend in the road to distract me.

My guts tighten. I'm about to break down and cry, but the rain eases and I can see patches of blue sky ahead. And a village or town not far away. My spirits soar as I enter the village and can see an odd-looking bell tower on the church. There are three bells in small arches, each holding up huge stork nests.

Café con leche. The potential for a sip of the aromatic warm greatness I have only recently discovered sends me on a mission. I search for a café or bar. It's still early. The first bar I find is full of chattering farmers staying in from their muddy fields.

I take a seat at a corner table by the window. While I wait for my coffee, I watch thin bands of rain mixed with patches of bright sunlight scurry across the town, down the streets, and over the nearby buildings.

After a second coffee I can't afford, I finally feel warmth slip into my toes again. Orbigo is only another ten miles. I hope the road will improve now that the sun has come out.

I pay for my coffees, put my raincoat back on, and, while the farmers watch in amazement, I pick up my pack and head for the door. I hope these men will pray for more sunshine on the path before me.

Astorga, Spain
September 14, 1982
Should I get my hopes up? I now have an address for Father, stumbled on it really. At the first worksite I came to I asked about him. A man there had worked with him recently. I will go to the place in the morning. If I have any luck, I'll take up private investigation. There must be a need for people to find their loved ones who have rushed out of their lives for one reason or another. But there I go, getting my hopes up.

From Georgia's Travel Journal

TWENTY-EIGHT

Astorga, October 31, 2019

The small, inexpensive albergue where I stayed last night had a little fire, with fifteen soaked-to-the-bone pilgrims crowded around it, all of us trying our best to get warm. The clothes dryer in a room close to my bunk went all evening and late into the night.

It's sunny now and the path in front of me dries slowly, vapors rising from the ground like from a cooling pot of stew. The number of puddles I must walk around become fewer and fewer as I reach the outskirts of Astorga and its paved streets.

I enter the city of 11,000 people, the feared goal, and my guts cannot possibly get more entwined. I taste bile in the back of my mouth.

On my smartphone, I have followed a red line into this city

and to the address I have searched for so many times before that I know it by heart. There's a café on my left, the nutty aroma of a fresh café con leche pulls at me. But my stomach could not handle it right now, nor my budget. Since León, I have budgeted my money, only spending nine euros for a bed last night, which included an amazing, blazing wood stove, and three more on a couple of energy bars to keep me moving forward, plus two coffees.

In the center of town, right where I expected, I find the central plaza, a chapel, a church, and behind them a cathedral climbs to the gray sky. At the Palace of Gaudi, I go right, toward and through a traffic circle, heading to the far edge of the city. At Calle de Oliegos, I take another right. As I near some tilled lands at the edge of the city, I come to a corner and to the street address I first saw on a manila envelope several weeks ago—the place where Georgia's journal is being sent from some nameless person.

On one side, an apartment building rises above the old red brick home. The dark, weathered oak door in front of me has the address above it, and a semi-circular balcony above. The window blinds are closed. The place seems lifeless.

In the center of the door hangs an iron knocker, a huge, heavy ring, and a thick block to drop it onto. The knocker is painted black, only slightly darker than the wooden door. The darkness of it feels like my insides. Cool and damp as the air seems, I perspire. Beads of sweat hang on my forehead. I slide the band of my cap down to soak up the droplets, then remove the hat, pull it from my ponytail, and grip it in one hand.

I should go and get cleaned up first. I'm sure I look horrible, the filthiest pilgrim to ever walk into Astorga. *Get on with it, girl.*

I step up to the door.

The iron clang vibrates through the heavy wood. I quickly drop it a second time and take a step backward.

Long seconds creep by. I want to turn and run, having done all I could. *Suck it up.*

I am here now, gotta stay put. I hear soft footsteps from inside. The doorknob turns, and the door creaks as the thick wood moves away from me. I still want to run. I came here. What more could Aunt Georgia and my grandmother want of me?

I smell freshly brewing coffee.

The door opens and the dim light of this gray day fills the entryway. When I see her, I almost fall over backward. My knees go weak. My backpack weighs heavy on my shoulders. There, right there in front of me, stands a spitting image of my mother. Darkness encircles my world, and I'm back on those tumbledown front steps at my parents' cabin in the woods. I take another step backward, turning left then right. As if through a thick gray bubble, I look up and down the street. A Spanish street.

The woman in the doorway is a healthier version of my mother, with beautiful skin the color of sage honey. But she looks otherwise exactly like Laura. She, too, looks lost in what or who stands in front of her.

She steps slightly forward. She also looks in both directions, can see I am alone.

The darkness fades away. A slight drizzle begins to fall on me. The woman looks into my eyes, looks deep into me for a long moment. Then I see it, a glimmer of understanding.

The puzzle pieces click together. This woman has sent Georgia's journal pages. She is family.

We stand there, speechless. My now-trembling body and almost useless mind find each other, try to work together again. I pull off my pack and stand it at my feet. I strip the rain cover from the top and open the pack. The first thing I come to is the protective sleeve with the journal inside. I draw it out, step closer to the woman and out of the misting rain, and slide Georgia's hand-written pages out for this woman to see.

She looks at them and back to me. She nods her head. "My name is Máire." I barely hear her, but the syllables of her name sounded as if they would rhyme with *boy* and *duh*. Which is exactly how I feel. "Please come inside, out of the rain," she says as she slips back into the home, the door opening wide.

Stupid. Why had I assumed she wouldn't speak English? "My name is Summer. I have come from California." Again, she nods.

I lift my pack and step inside.

Máire looks out to the street again, then closes the door. "Set your things here," she says as she nods toward a corner of the entryway. She points into a dark room filled with chairs and a large sofa. "You have come a long way. Please take a seat."

"My clothes are wet, I'm muddy."

She takes my rain jacket and waits while I remove my filthy shoes. "I will hang this here, by the door," she says. The jacket drips on its way to the hook of a hall tree. She sets the muddy shoes on a newspaper on the floor and goes for a towel.

After wiping off what I can, I sit on the edge of the sofa, my toes cold. The sofa is old and worn but covered with a beautiful tapestry material.

Máire returns and turns on a table lamp. The light is weak but warm, inviting. "Would you like some coffee, Summer?" she asks. Her tone says to me she's trying my name on for size.

"Yes, please," I say.

From the kitchen through a doorway to my left, Máire says, "They named me after my grandmother. She was from Galicia, the region not far from here. The name has a Gaelic spelling and meaning. I will write them down for you. How did you get to Astorga?"

"I walked the Camino de Santiago, followed Georgia's diary. Followed her father . . ."

Máire sets a cup with dark, rich liquid on a table at my side.

I watch wisps of steam float up from the cup, my nerves

wanting to release. She returns to her seat. This woman is not a fiery demon, not an angel packing around a human skull, not a faceless creature in a black cloak, none of the things I had imagined.

"He was my grandfather," Máire says.

"I have only met my Grandma Pat, his daughter," I say. "Aunt Georgia died when I was little."

She puts a hand to her chest and bows her head for a moment, then says, "Grandfather died many years ago when I was about your age. I know he came here from California. I know what Georgia wrote in her journal," says Máire as she gets up and steps to a cabinet under the front window. She opens a shallow drawer and removes a leather folder. She pulls out a short stack of familiar looking pages and brings them to me. "I had hoped someone would write to me. Ask for these last pages."

I look up and into her now moist eyes. She grieves too. I see other emotions. Guilt? She hands me the last few pages of the journal. I take them. She steps away.

"You sent the others to my grandmother. I lived with her, came to Spain with her."

Máire sits on the other end of the sofa, sighs, and sits back. "Not long before my mother died, she told me about my family in America, gave me the journal. I didn't know what to do with it."

I push back into the soft sofa, sip on the hot coffee, delaying. I don't know what to say. I came here with questions. She is the one with the answers.

"My grandmother married a man from California. She was lonely. He was lonely. Mother told me over and over how much they came to love one another. They made a life here, raised a family. She was my grandmother, also named Máire, as I said. He was Abuelo Harold, or Grandfather Harold."

"Harold," I say, realizing I have never used his name. I knew it, of course, but never thought of him with a proper name. "And Samantha, my great-grandmother, his . . . his first wife."

Máire starts to weep. She pulls a tissue from a box on the side table and dries her eyes. "I am sorry, Summer. You came to Spain. I made you walk to Astorga . . . I . . ." She stops and straightens. "How old are you, child?"

Used to guarding this information, I hesitate, then answer her. "Sixteen."

"And you walked to here. You said you came to Europe with your grandmother?" she says. It's a question. A big one. *The* big one.

"Yes. We started the Camino del Norte like Georgia did, where she did. We hiked to San Sebastián," I say and stop there. The painful memory rushes in on me. As the miles went by on the Camino, and while making friends in two different Camino families, the day—now weeks ago—had faded. But I see her pale, peaceful face again. There in my final embrace.

Máire is now the quiet one. The one waiting for answers to come forward. She picks up her coffee cup, blows away some of its heat.

"She died in the cathedral in San Sebastián." Máire gasps, sets her coffee aside. My head hangs low, the fragrant wisps of coffee rising to my face, teardrops falling into the cup. "In the Cathedral of the Buen Pastor. A heart attack, they said."

She comes to my side. "What have I done?"

I know what she has done. But I don't know how it makes me feel. Was it wrong? Máire did not kill my grandmother, her weak heart did.

We sit quietly for a long time, her soft hands wrapped around mine where they sit on my lap, still wrapped around the coffee cup.

Slowly, she releases her grip and stands. She walks to a wall across the dark room. I had not seen them before, but there are several framed pictures hanging on the wall. She removes one from its hook and brings it back to the sofa. She sits again. I set my cup down. We both hold the picture frame.

"This is me," she says as she points to a girl in a dark blue dress. "And this man... our Grandfather Harold."

The tears come again. I dry mine with a sleeve.

He's muscular and handsome and has a gloomy face. The slightly upturned corners of his mouth look flat, like he has forgotten how to smile. His eyes look sad, like he knows it but can't help it. One of his arms rests draped around the girl's narrow shoulders.

"Why did you send Georgia's journal? And why only some of it at a time?" I ask.

Máire sits quietly for a moment, reflecting, reviewing her decisions. "My grandparents lived in this very same home. The place where Georgia found her father. Where she stayed with him and my grandmother for a time. She had the upstairs bedroom. Abuelo Harold worked for a builder here in Astorga. He became a mason, learned the trade on his own, I was told. Before he died, many people came to seek his advice about their projects. Grandmother had a flower stand not far from here. It is still in operation today. My mother, their only child, was born here. She and father had an apartment," she says, then sniffles and dries her eyes again.

I'm as weak as a sick dog, wanting answers, also to scurry away, return to the Camino, find my peace. I wish Grandma Pat were here, yet I know she is.

Máire collects more pictures from the wall. She sits beside me. "These are my parents. This photo was taken the summer before they were killed in an automobile accident, two years ago, now." She sniffles again and wipes her nose with a new tissue.

She only lets me hold the picture for a few seconds, taking it back and tenderly setting it in her lap.

"Are there any pictures of Georgia, from when she stayed here?"

She thinks about my question for a short moment and says, "You know, I have never seen one, never seen her. I have this image of her from reading her journal. It seems so clear in my mind. She was pretty, wasn't she?"

"Yes. Very."

We sit quietly for long, uncomfortable minutes.

"More coffee?" she asks.

Before answering, I look to the window. The remaining daylight already weakening. "I should get going. I plan to hike to Rechi . . . Reki. . ."

"Murias de Rechivaldo."

"Yes, that's it."

"Would you like to see his grave? Your Grandfather Harold's resting place?" she asks.

"I guess so," I say, not sure I do. *You have come this far.*

"Summer," she says and looks directly into my eyes. "You are welcome to stay the night. Stay here; use Georgia's room. We could go to the *cementerio* in the morning. You can return to the Camino afterward, in the afternoon. I know someone who has an albergue in Rechivaldo. She is a good friend. I can call Priscilla and tell her you are coming."

The ugly truth is, the first thing I think of, following Máire's offer, is the money I can save and my hopes for ruining Tilly's horrible plan.

It's after eight o'clock now. I've cleaned up and hung everything to dry in the bedroom where Georgia once lived. I step into the kitchen. Máire gives a pot of beans a quick stir. As she pours wine in our glasses, I pull my phone from my back pocket. I should let Lou know what is going on. At least part of it, what I know. She knew each day I hiked closer to where those envelopes came from.

I begin tapping out the message.
I have the rest of Georgia's journal.
You won't believe what else I have found.
What else should I tell her?
I will call you tomorrow on Skype.

She'll want to kill me for not calling her right now. But I don't know everything, not yet.

Will call you before I leave Astorga.

Astorga, Spain
September 15, 1982

Father wasn't happy when, after answering the door, I told him who I was. Before that moment, I couldn't remember his face. But when he stepped into the light, peering through his doorway, I knew it was him immediately. He may have thought it a joke at first, though he did not smile. He would have left me there and closed the door in my face. But his… his woman… she made him bring me in and explain what was going on. She did not know about his family in the US.

From Georgia's Travel Journal

TWENTY-NINE

Astorga, November 1, 2019

It's dark when I wake, eerily quiet. This is the time of day I usually prepare for another long walk.

Yesterday returns to my thoughts. I allow them to cast shadows over what I would rather be doing right now. Máire is an excellent cook. Late into the evening we ate and talked and sat quietly for long moments, each of us organizing the true and complete story of our family in our minds. Repeatedly she had asked about Grandma Pat, how she had died. She wept each time. I hugged her, she hugged me back.

I turn to my side and slowly swing my legs off the bed and sit up. The wine she served and kept pouring throughout the evening causes a hammer to pound away in my skull. Thank goodness she added water to my wine glass.

From downstairs I hear a thud and the sound of running water. I sit there on the edge of the bed, listening. My body complains some more. Besides my headache, my legs have an irritating itch to go, to walk, to leave this city behind. I found Máire. Walking to Santiago will come next.

At the wall closest to me sits an old vanity, its mirror checked with a brown stain behind the beveled glass. A chair is there too, matching the dark reddish brown of the vanity. Georgia sat there fixing her hair or writing in her journal. Why did she leave the journal behind? Last night I could only read a few lines from the pages Máire gave to me before I fell into a deep sleep. I will read the rest of her story very soon.

Wisps of brewing coffee enter the room. They wrap around me, stand me up, and urge me to get dressed. Before going downstairs, I pull back the window blinds to look outdoors and up and down the street. This is where they lived and worked. This became their life, Grandma Pat. We found him, my great-grandfather Harold, your father. His Spanish family, his Spanish granddaughter, who looks incredibly like my mother, your daughter. There is no question they are related, we are related.

Did Grandfather Harold find peace here in his new life? Did he ever question what he had done? Did he worry about having two wives? And how did his new wife feel about it once she knew? Did she have suspicions about an American family before Georgia showed up on their doorstep in 1982? And how did that evening's conversation go?

I came here for answers, only to have more questions. Young Máire knows some of those answers. She has read Georgia's journal to her very last entry.

Now dressed, I go downstairs. I stop in the doorway to the kitchen. Máire stands busy at the counter. Does her head hurt as bad as mine? Another question.

"Ah, you are up early," Máire says, then realizes something. She shakes her head and says, "You are a pilgrim now. Coffee?"

"I can get it," I say as I reach for a cup on the counter.

"Here," she says as she opens a cupboard door. "You look like you could use a larger one." She hands me a cup the size of my favorite one at home, back in California. In a little place called Julian, where they grow apples and bake pies to have with your coffee. Will I ever drink tea again? Questions.

"He found peace here, didn't he?" I say as I pour the dark brown goodness into my cup. "Grandfather Harold."

"I like to think so. I didn't know of his past until I read Georgia's story. But I have memories of good times with him and my grandmother."

"Why did Georgia leave her journal behind when she left Astorga?"

"Read it to the end. You will learn what I have. Georgia would want it that way," Máire declares as she brings long pieces of *tostada*, toasted fresh bread, to the table. She points to a bottle on the table and says, "Try the olive oil. It comes from a farm near here. They, the farmer, and his wife, were friends of my parents. We will go to the cemetery after you are ready if you want."

"Yes, of course."

After another long soak in the tub, I come back downstairs. We get our coats, step outside and she locks the door. "The cemetery is not far. We will buy flowers on our way."

I feel clean and I don't stink for the first time in weeks. Máire even wiped my backpack and shoes clean. She probably did these things because I lay forever in the tub, soaking in warm, sudsy water where Georgia did the same so many years ago.

I walk now without a backpack and feel like a butterfly, light and unburdened. My feet don't seem to touch the ground, not like they are accustomed to when we start our usual day on the

Camino. Máire walks slowly but purposefully. I often slow my pace to match her steady stride.

"When Georgia walked the Camino, and when her father did so before her, the experience was very different."

"Yes. Many pilgrims walk the Camino these days," she says. "I didn't tell you, did I? I walked the Way from here to Sarria once. I met Priscilla on that trek." She looks at me. I don't remember who Priscilla is, a fact certainly showing on my face. "Ah, the woman at the private albergue in Murias. I called her while you bathed." She was busy this morning. "Priscilla expects you this evening. It is not far, only a few kilometers beyond Astorga."

"A private albergue?" I ask, while my mind again goes through the hard work of math.

"Yes?" she says, with a questioning tone.

"I only have. . ." I'm embarrassed to say. But it's all Tilly's fault. "I don't have much money to get me to Santiago."

"Tonight, it has been taken care of for you. Now you have more money than you thought."

"I don't know what to say." Though I do: *Take that, Tilly.*

"Nothing needs said. The Camino provides. Sometimes friends and family do as well."

Her words remind me of Father Ernesto. He had said those words, "The Camino provides." I have heard other people say the same thing, sometimes in different ways. And I know it's true. It has been true for a thousand years, true for my great-grandfather and my great-aunt. I remember the Camino gave me Beth and Howard, and they gave me Eunate, and that experience literally changed the way I see the world around me. The hippies I grew up around called it aura. "Everything has an aura," they would say. I thought them simply crazy or high or both.

"Will you walk to Santiago someday?" I ask.

"Here, the flowers, the stall my grandmother owned for many years," says Máire, seeming to ignore my question.

The lady at the stall hands Máire a bundle of flowers. She gives the woman a few euro coins. They don't say a word during this short exchange.

"The cemetery is close, now. This way," she says, pointing toward a side street.

We enter the grounds from Calle Nigrillo and walk beside a wall. Before coming to a gateway on our right, Máire turns left. We stop at the first set of graves. They are rectangular crypts made of polished stone, similar in size to those nearby. "These are my parents, Fernando and Selena." She removes dried old flowers from a glass vase on each vault and hands them to me. With a cloth she has taken from her coat pocket she dusts the ornate stone and lovingly cleans out the engravings. She pulls a few of the new flowers from her bundle and divides them between the two graves.

She moves to the foot of the crypts, bows, and says a prayer under her breath. I feel so sad for her. I have living parents, yet I tell people they are dead. *You can fix that, girl.*

Finished here, she guides me through the opening in the wall we had been following. "This is the older part of the cemetery," she tells me.

"It's huge. The area inside these walls could hold half of the town where I live," I say, before thinking my words somehow inappropriate.

"Much history lies here. Wealthy families. Founders of the original town. And the poor. All catholic." As we continue down an aisle, she leans into me like a spy on a mission. "We will not mention Abuelo Harold's American wife. Yes?"

"Sure, I guess." *Who would I mention her to?* I wonder as I look around and see no one else but us two.

She leads right and then left. Under the shade of a tall tree beside a huge mausoleum with a domed roof, she stops. "There he is, on the left," she says as she points toward the taller crypt of two within a short, wrought-iron fence. She waits for me to step close.

I step through an opening at the front of the fenced area. There he rests. I had never considered the possibility of coming this close to him. Grandma Pat had, I suppose, but the thought hadn't come to me, ever.

Flowers in a silver vase hang dead and dried. I remove them and dust their remains from the polished dark stone. I read his name and the dates of his troubled life chiseled into the polished granite. I know now he had found peace.

I turn, stooping to read his Spanish wife's details before making room for Máire the younger to complete her routine chore.

I have never felt this somber before. Sad as I felt then, there was no time for grieving when Grandma Pat died. Too many issues to consider, too much needing done. Now I feel the weight of it all. It pulls at me; I wish I had a chair to collapse into.

Máire has finished her duties. "We can stay as long as you like." She takes the dead flowers from me.

"Can I take a picture?" I ask, still uncertain about proper decorum.

"Yes, of course, an excellent idea." She says, then steps back to his crypt and sweeps away a tiny speck of something I had not seen. "Remember, though, you can come and visit him anytime. Please know this."

"Thank you. I will." I pull out my smartphone and wake it up. As I lift the device up, my world goes fuzzy. My view is from inside again, like I am behind the camera's lens, and it needs to focus. I can't move. I feel them here. Grandfather Harold, Aunt Georgia, and Grandma Pat are with us. I feel my knees weaken. I'm about to collapse when Máire steadies me. Their lives roll before the camera. Battles and beaches, swimming pools and trains, apple pies and smoke-filled kitchens, miles of the Camino in a different light, at a different time.

I have no idea how long it has been, but I eventually straighten like a recently watered flower. Máire gives me space, doesn't say a word about what has happened. She probably has no clue what to say. I finally snap a few pictures with the phone and confirm I have one I like.

Máire comes close again and stands in front of me. I reach out and we take each other in our arms. It's a long, warm, tender, emotion-driven embrace before we release.

As we walk out of the cemetery, I realize I have known this woman for less than a day, and I know very little about her. But we are family.

We say our goodbyes at the door to Máire's home, the family home. We have made our promises to write one another, promises I hope we can keep. I, too, without having any concept of where I will live, have invited her to come visit us in America anytime she wants. At this she says nothing, only nodding her head as she slips back through the door and closes it.

I turn away and head back to the plaza to find splashes of yellow paint on light poles and brass markers of the Camino de Santiago in the sidewalks. As I walk along the streets of this lovely city I had once feared, I recall my promise to Lou. I'll call her before I've gone too far, and the cell signal gets too weak.

After finding my route out of town and quieter streets, I open the Skype app and call Lou's number. I hope she's up this early in California—and alone. The connection completes and I see her smiling face. She's not in her room; I'm not sure where she is. "Hey, Louise."

"Don't call me that," says Lou before she bursts into laughter, which rolls into a giggling session, one I involuntarily join. We giggle like little girls for a half a minute or more before I ask where she is. Her face is so close to the phone I can't make anything out.

Lou pulls her phone back and says, "I'm in the kitchen. Mom isn't up yet. I'm working on breakfast and finishing homework at the same time." Homework. I've completely forgotten about schoolwork. "So, what did you find?"

"Not only what, but whom," I say. Lou grins at me and tilts her head. "I found the rest of Georgia's journal. And our family."

"Wait, what? Is he alive?" she asks with a serious note. "And what more does the journal say, and about *whom*?" She smiles into her phone's camera again.

"He died long ago, Lou. I met his granddaughter. She's sort of a half-cousin, I guess. You wouldn't believe it; she looks like my mother. And she's super nice." There I go again calling things *super*. "She invited me to stay over last night and to visit our grandfather's grave this morning. He's been gone for many years now. We went to the cemetery and put out new flowers and everything." Though I don't tell her everything.

"You're lucky," she says, and her brilliant smile fills the screen again.

"Let me tell you about the—"

"Summer. Is that you?" asks a grating, ugly, all-too-familiar voice.

The image from Lou's phone goes wobbly and Tilly's round face fills my screen.

"Yes. Good morning, Tilly." Which is all I can say, having hoped to avoid this encounter.

"You need to come home, come home right now, young lady."

At this, and the suddenness of her attack, I feel my blood begin to seethe. It's about to boil. I grin into the phone's camera.

"I'm fine, thanks for asking. Oh, and I had a wonderful birthday. We had a party and everything."

"Look, you little shit,"—I deserve this one—"there are things to take care of here. And I'm not doing them on my own. Get your ass on the next plane home." She's getting red in the face, her eyes squinting.

"I'm almost done here. I'll come home as scheduled. I'll be in Santiago in a week or so from now. Then I'll take the flights home Grandma Pat had booked for me."

"Look. . ." Here we go again. "Summer, you are only a child. You need to come home. I am responsible for you now."

"Not yet. I'm almost done here."

"You selfish little—"

"I found your father, Aunt Tilly. I found Grandfather Harold."

She's quiet for a long moment. I see Lou reach for the phone. Tilly wrenches it back and says, "Why should I care? He left me. Before I was even born. He. Left. Me."

There it is. The man left her, no one else but her. How sad.

"I'll come home as planned," I repeat. *And there's nothing you can do about it.* Except what she has already done.

The image of her on the screen shakes, and her face becomes even redder than before. Through gritted teeth she says, "You need to get your ass on a bus right now."

"I can't do that. Remember, you did something to Grandma Pat's debit card. All her cards. I have very little money. I can't do anything more than walk to Santiago—as planned."

She stays silent for another moment. I think she's going to cry. Without another word, she hands the phone back to Lou. I can't see her now, but I watch as Lou's eyes follow her mother out of the kitchen.

"Are you okay?" asks Lou.

"Ugh, that woman. Yeah, I'm fine. But I need to finish this.

We finish what we started, right?" I see Lou's head nod in silent agreement. "But I don't know if I can," I say as my reality sinks deeper into my heart.

"What do you mean? You can do this. I know you can." She pauses for a second. "Oh, the money?"

"I don't have enough." The words have slipped from my mouth. I want them back. This is not Lou's fault, not her problem.

"What did she do?"

I hesitate, not knowing how to stop the flow of anger I feel right now. "Your mother turned off Grandma Pat's credit cards, did something so they won't work." I see profound irritation on my cousin's face, one I had never imagined possible. "Sorry, Lou."

She's speechless. I'm mad at myself.

"I'm so sorry, Lou," I say again.

"Me too," she says. With no more to say, we say our goodbyes and kill the connection.

Astorga, Spain

September 16, 1982

I looked, stared if I'm honest, at Máire's belly, and realized my curiosity. That's when father confirmed her pregnancy. I don't know if he would have said otherwise. "Boy or girl," I asked, though he could not know. He shrugged and said, "Father Luis says it's a boy. But he always says, 'It shall be a male child.' He's right half the time—better than most." So, I will have a half sister or brother.

From Georgia's Travel Journal

THIRTY

Murias de Rechivaldo, November 2, 2019

As quietly as possible I climb down the outside stairs and cross the gravel patio. The crunch of my footsteps seems loud enough to wake the entire village. Lights from the kitchen spill onto the ground. Priscilla greets me at the doorway. It's cold outside and already smells like rain. From inside, familiar aromas of bread baking in a hot oven tug at me. My knees nearly buckle, but I need to get going. It will be a very long—and treacherous, if I believe what Priscilla has told me—route over the mountains to the town of Molinaseca.

"Are you ready to go?"

"Yes," I say without much enthusiasm. "Thank you for listening to me last night. I guess I needed to let out the fiery anger my aunt lit off inside of me."

"No problema, chica," she says with a tender smile. As soon

as I had entered her albergue the evening before and told her my name, we became fast friends. She said I reminded her of her good friend Máire. Priscilla says my new-found cousin's name with a forceful, guttural tone and a phlegmy finish I'd love to master. She tried to help me learn, but said I need *mucho* practice.

Standing here now, I wish I could take back all those things I told her about Aunt Tilly. But the words—all of them true—spilled out of my mouth. I could no longer hold them back.

"Remember to watch for the storm," Priscilla says as she looks into my eyes with the seriousness of a guardian. "They say much rain comes our way. And cold will enter the high mountains. You must take caution."

I nod my head as she hands me a huge sandwich wrapped in aluminum foil. The sandwich, the shape of a thick, square block, weighs at least a pound. While I load it into a pouch on my backpack and pull the rain cover back over, Priscilla bundles herself against the cool morning air in a colorful shawl. She stands before me with that look again, like she's torn between wanting to wrap me in her arms to hold me here and knowing I need to go.

"There are many villages along your route," she begins. "You do not need to put yourself in danger, do not need to trek all the way at once. All forty kilometers. In miles, how many is that?"

"Twenty-four," I say, while I know damn well I'm fudging a distance closer to twenty-five miles." Deceit comes easier the more I use the practice, even with math.

"Ay. Take careful steps, my young friend," she says before tearing herself away and returning to the warmth of her kitchen.

I buckle up my pack and walk through the portico and out to the street. The little town ends after Priscilla's place. Beyond, only the Camino de Santiago as it enters tree-studded grasslands. A wind howls toward me from the west. Tall grasses sway and bend on blast after blast of damp air. My cheeks and my knees tingle from the cold. I pull up my collar and tug down on my cap. Wishing they wouldn't, my eyes look to the horizon. From there, they lift higher and higher following gray, billowing storm clouds toward the stratosphere.

I can hear Tilly's voice on the wind and see her angry face in those clouds. She was so upset with me yesterday I can imagine her summoning this storm. I also wish I could talk with her, really talk with her, help her understand.

My trail day begins.

One idyllic village after another comes and goes as I keep to a quick pace. During a clear day, and if I had the time, I'd love to stay for a while and sip on café con leches in each of these towns. Most have an albergue and a bar, as Priscilla had told me. Like my new friend Sara had considered a few days ago, "I could settle down right here and find happiness." And I think I could, almost. The peace and quiet soaks into your bones during the beautiful days. But today, it will rain. The cold already seeps in, finding its way through the layers and into my bones.

I started off in shorts this morning. Why, I'm not sure. But my bare legs haven't complained too much. Their work keeps them warm.

It starts to drizzle, winds gusting across the tilted countryside.

After a dozen miles, the Camino begins to climb well into the mountains ahead. I come to the old village of Foncebadón. I say "old," but they're all old. This one, though, has a broken-down, crumbling look about it. There are newer places built because of the pilgrim trade. But there are many walls dwindling into old age.

Beside the main street sits a bar. A few determined looking pilgrims sit under a thin metal awning. The bar looks busy inside, but I'm getting cold and need a dry place to eat the sandwich Priscilla made for me.

I step through the door and get immediately slammed by the

noisy din of conversation and laughter. All the tables have seated customers. I'm about to shoot back out the door and explore other options when a middle-aged man comes over to say I should sit with him and his friends; they have room at their table. The warmth tugs on me. Guess I'll stay.

Talk centers on the weather. Forecasts get shared and analyzed. They are ignored by some and clearly feared by others.

"I'm finding a place here to stay," says an older woman. She has a German accent.

"We go on," says an Italian man at a nearby table with his two companions.

"Is anyone going as far as Molinaseca today?" I ask as I look around.

People at surrounding tables quiet down and look my way. Many shaking their heads, not even considering the possibility. A few say things like, "We shall see," and "Perhaps." I settle on these words, *hitch my wagon to them*, as Grandma Pat would have said.

Eventually, the crowd thins. Only a drizzle falls from the sky, and I decide it's time to go. Since I have a place to sit and put on my rain pants, I give the idea quick consideration. But no, "I should get going," I whisper to myself.

Full, rested, and riding on a bit of caffeine, I hit the trail at full speed. The climb resumes as soon as the Camino does. Upward I go, following a few poncho-clad pilgrims up ahead. We all try to beat the worst of the storm—by racing toward it.

The wind dies, and real raindrops begin to fall. They intensify. In a few short moments the trail becomes a river of muddy water. I can still see those tougher pilgrims up the trail from me. They pull me along as if I'm in their slipstream. The nascent river course gets slippery. I'm trying to walk on the high sides of the trail to keep my feet as dry as possible. At times, I slip and slide more than I make forward progress. Thank goodness I have my trekking poles, or I'd sprawl out like a slithering otter. Take careful steps, Priscilla had said.

The Camino comes to a stretch of paved road leading off into the gray. I no longer see the walking ponchos. I turn and look back. No one there either.

I keep climbing. The rain eases. The air gets colder by the minute.

Leaning over my phone to block the raindrops from its screen, I check my location. I'm near Cruz de Ferro, though I can't see a thing but the road and a few trees and bushes beside the path. The blue dot in the app, me, on the red line, the Camino, are all that matter right now. This would not be a good time to get lost.

Should have listened to Priscilla.

Finally, I see the image I have seen in pictures many times since first learning about the Camino de Santiago. A huge pile of stones looms beside the road, a tall staff spiking up from the top, and an iron cross, which I can barely see through the fog, atop the staff. You are meant to bring a stone from home, one to represent all your troubles. When you get here, you throw the stone and your problems on the stack with everyone else's. I don't have a stone. The trouble I have right now turns to snowflakes.

Sleet floods down my jacket and from my sleeves. My knees are red from the cold. Snowflakes begin to stick to the ground. The worst of it, though, is my hands. I have on the thin gloves Grandma Pat told me to bring, but they are soaking wet. I can't put my hands in my pockets because I need to use my poles while walking the slippery trails.

I look up to the cross one last time and ask Father Ernesto to say a word or two for me.

The Camino stays to the road for a while longer before returning to narrow rivulets of mud. It takes me a while to figure out that the trail parallels the paved road much of the time.

Where I can, I stay on the pavement and watch my Camino app to make sure I'm on course.

This, unfortunately, does not last and I'm back on muddy, wet rocks. My shoes don't want to grip the gray stone in this rotten weather. I have no choice but to keep going. My legs are cold, knees now wobbly from hunger and the cold and the miles. I pass a Camino marker with the distance to Santiago and slowly do the math. Now I know I'm close to Molinaseca, today's destination.

The ugly trail drops to a paved lane. I celebrate, hoping I've seen the last of those wet trails and muddy streams for this day.

The rain slows and the fog lifts as I walk to the edge of town. I turn left and cross a stone bridge. At the other side of the river is heaven. Buildings line the narrow streets. A few people walk quickly here or there. To save as much money as possible, I plan to stay at the municipal albergue—beyond the far side of town.

Even in the mist, the quiet streets, the buildings bending over them, and the worn block-paved path I walk on are stunning. The ambiance is so amazing I think I've found my new favorite Spanish village. As tired as I am, I find myself standing in front of an ancient block-built structure that has crumbled and been repaired with rough stones and whatever may have been handy at the time. A block arch surrounds a wood door of craggy, gray oak.

I start walking again. Business signs stick out overhead, each vying with those next to them. Some of the signs are faded and weathered, probably older than my grandmother. Others are new, with bright LED lights blinking a symbol of one kind or another.

As I walk with as much power as my worn-out legs can provide, I pass a private albergue I had seen on my Camino app. A simple placard says they are full for the night. A couple blocks farther on, and in what looks like an older part of town, I come to another place closed for the season.

I tremble at the thought and curse Tilly for making this day more difficult than it needs to be. The thought of her warms my blood, not in a good way.

Today's walk took longer than I'd hoped, but the rain has nearly stopped and there's only a slight breeze when I reach the muni. It's a block building, under a huge roofline stretching well beyond the walls of the place. It looks inviting.

I climb the thankfully few steps and am about to reach for the door's handle when I see the dreaded and plastic-coated sign, *COMPLETO*. They even put this one in all caps. Dammit.

I can't sleep in a closet again, won't beg for mercy. I go back to the road and look west. It's too far to the next town, Ponferrada. So, around I go, heading back into Molinaseca. I feel Tilly here, laughing at me. Adding to this horrible thought, the skies unleash, and rain pours down again. I'm going to strangle the old, spiteful hag.

Astorga, Spain
September 18, 1982
What a gorgeous day. We spent the morning at the weekly market in the plaza. When everyone went to enjoy their afternoon siesta, I visited a palace designed by Anton Gaudi. He is famous here in Spain for his unique designs. After that, I toured the cathedral before visiting a chocolate museum. An actual museum—just for chocolate. Oh, and samples too.

From Georgia's Travel Journal

THIRTY-ONE

Molinaseca, November 3, 2019

At the road, and disappointed at turning back, I pull up my collar once again and begin to walk easterly. I no longer need my trekking poles and strap them to my pack, then tug the pack cover down to the hip belt. My hands now free, I place them in the pockets of my raincoat. Immediately, they begin to sting and tingle from the new-found warmth.

The rain pours from the sky like a national park waterfall. I should have listened to Priscilla. In a few minutes I'm back to the old part of town. I concentrate on its beauty, trying to ignore the weakness in my body. Anger seeps in. *Tilly.*

She will not win. I can't let her. *No frickin' way.* When will she understand what I am trying to do here?

I need to find a way to convince Tilly to help me finish what her sisters had set out to do, and I need to read the rest of Georgia's journal. It cannot tell me if she ever got to Santiago. It may tell me what she planned for after Astorga, though.

With no other options, I start looking for a pensión or casa rurales for the night. The cost will further drain my money belt. *Dammit.* Before I know it, I've come to the other side of the village, back where I had started. All the places have been full. Completo.

A short man in a huge yellow raincoat comes my way. I step into his path.

"Peregrina?" he asks.

"Sí. Yo necessito una cama por la noche," I say in stuttering Spanish through chattering teeth. I can see him analyzing my words, translating the mess into something he can understand.

"Ah, sí, señorita. Casa Rurales Maria," he says and points into the clouds across the river. "Posiblemente."

I thank him and cross the river again. On the far side, I turn left, away from the Camino route I followed into this town. In a block or two I come to a huge brick-built home. The casa rurales sits above the road, up a long, wide staircase. At the top of the stairs, I don't see any lights on or signs of life, only a horrible placard. *Cerrado*, closed.

I sit on the steps under the roof covering the wide porch. I'm shivering. Water drips on my rosy knees and tingling hands. Much of the water falls cold, some of the drops are warm. I'm so cold I didn't realize I was crying until this moment. Will I freeze to death here on these red bricks? I could curl up in my sleeping bag against the wall, out of the rain. My teeth clatter like a machine gun. My knees bang against one another like frozen hands trying to clap.

Through the weakening light and heavy rain, I see a dark figure hurrying along the street. I run, stumble, nearly fall onto the street. The person stops. She is tall and pretty under thick layers of coats and a shimmering green and blue scarf. She can see my predicament.

"Come with me," she says in accented English. I follow.

We walk back into the village, twisting and turning for a few blocks before stopping.

"This is my cousin's pensión. She will find you a bed for the night and something to dry you off."

What will this place cost? *Does it matter? You want to freeze to death?* So many stupid questions.

The lady opens the door and calls out, "Rosita?"

Another woman with the similarly tall features comes from a back room, wiping her hands on a white cotton towel.

"Do you have a bed for this one?" asks her cousin.

"Ah, another drowned pilgrim. Sí."

I stand there dripping, melting from the long day, the storm, and my aunt. I'm almost helpless. No, I *am* helpless.

The two women help me take off my backpack and remove the outer layers which did not serve too well to keep me dry today.

Rosita says goodbye to her cousin and leads me to a registration desk. I'm still shivering; she doesn't seem to notice. She points to a sign on the wall behind her. Thirty-three euros for the night. I want to weep. I pull up my shirt to access my money belt. I open it and cherish the few bills still there. When I finish paying for tonight's room, I see much more open space than bills in the pouch clinging to the clammy skin of my belly.

Our transaction complete, Rosita guides me upstairs. She unlocks the door to my room, hands me the key, then shows me to the large restroom on this floor. She opens a cupboard and hands me a bath towel. Looking at me with a funny grin, her hand pushes back the restroom door to reveal a clawfoot bathtub. *OMG, heaven.* She turns on the water, makes sure the liquid coming from the spout flows hot, then leaves me to it. I don't care about the cost of the room anymore. I will work it off if I have to.

I soak in the tub until the water becomes too cold to enjoy any longer. After wringing out rainwater from everything I wore today, and rinsing out a few things, I dig through my pack and find dry shorts and a top.

Back in my room, I burrow under the covers and pull my backpack close, trying to find something to eat in there. The breakfast included in the price of this room is hours away. My empty stomach grumbles. Too bad Beth and Cheryl are not here to laugh at me.

Warm now, and mostly happy, the idea of how many times I have thought I would sleep outside comes to me. Again, the Camino brought to me what I needed when I needed it most. There's still a nagging question: What can I do about Tilly?

Astorga, Spain
September 19, 1982

Máire asked me to help her with dinner last night. What a disaster. She was patient with me, though I am certain I doubled her workload. Too many dirty dishes, flour, and messes everywhere. I will never make it as a chef. Father simply grinned and shrugged his shoulders at her distress over my latest spill or faux pas. He clearly loves her. Only tolerates me. And he says we need to talk.

From Georgia's Travel Journal

THIRTY-TWO

Molinaseca, November 4, 2019

My gourmet granola bar dinner has gone long ago, if it registered at all in my digestive system.

Right now, I'm so hungry the wonderfully layered aromas of coffee brewing don't compete with whatever is in the oven. *Rosita, open it already!*

I'm the first of her clients seated in the dining room. Through an open door, I can see Rosita moving about. My gastric organs flinch and abdominal muscles ripple. A youngish couple arrive and take a little table by the window. They look like Spanish tourists, though I wonder why they chose this time of year to visit the area. But then, why am I here? We all have some sort of plan, I suppose.

More people stream down the stairs and into the room. Time creeps by. Rosita finally brings out an urn of coffee. During her next trip she brings out tostada and pastries. Oh, yeah, here we go. Fast as *Silver Surfer*, I'm at the platter loading a plate with toasted baguettes and pastries with chocolate inside them. Faster still, my plate sits empty. Now I can have some coffee or tea. The tea selection is brilliant: An Earl Grey blend catches my eye. I leave it to steep at my table and return for more carbs. Rosita brings out scrambled eggs. *Oh, yeah.*

My eggs are gone, and the platter is once again empty. All the tostada has disappeared. One more half-smashed pastry rests on its platter. My eyes focus on it, ignoring everyone else in the room. I'm about to get up when a woman pilgrim with large brown eyes and short hair comes to my table. She grins at me and sets a full plate of food in front of me.

My questioning eyes and tilted head convey words held in my throat.

"Fixed it for my husband. He's not here yet. Enjoy," she says and walks back to her table. Other guests around us grin at the woman's offering. I've made a pig of myself. Well, not yet.

A flush of embarrassment drives its way up my face. I think I thanked her. She goes back to her plate and cup of coffee and looks out one of the windows. I look at the plate, not wanting to take the man's breakfast. But she said to. I dig in, hoping to finish and leave the room before he joins her.

I was so occupied with eating, I hadn't yet looked outside. When I do, I'm happy to see sunlight, lots of it. My things can dry out as the day progresses. I thank Rosita and walk out into the day. Birds happily chirp. I buckle my backpack across my waist and chest and find my way back to the Camino.

A few other pilgrims already leave town ahead of me. I follow along and wonder if these people came over the summit near Cruz de Ferro in yesterday's horrible mess. Fluffy clouds hang on the mountain tops and ridge lines above this long river valley. It's a few delightful miles on a beautiful day to the next town, Ponferrada. I text Lou that I am fine; I will call in a day or two. Beth texts me at the same time. She says the gang is in Ponferrada and asks where I am. How in the world has this all worked out? Oh, well. I text back and say I'm not far away.

Walking a steady pace, and as I gawk at the lush green landscape still dripping from last night's heavy rains, a gurgling muddy river slips by on my right. Before long I can see the city and cross a bridge leading into an older part of town. The roads are busy, and the sidewalks filled with people beginning their day. Cheryl has texted me they are at the first restaurant I will come to, across from a Templar castle. I also remember seeing photos of that castle. I have read in recent weeks about the Templars after they came to Spain in the 1300s and started protecting people during their pilgrimages to Santiago.

Phil sees me first and calls to the others. He is busking—a term unknown to me until meeting Phil and his dangling dreads. He sits cross-legged at the edge of the sidewalk. Cheryl and Deanna stand at their table and wave me in their direction. Tiny, quiet-as-a-mouse Celeste sits beside Cheryl, Yan in the shadows. Phil sets down his guitar, gets up with ease, and gives me a tight hug, saying "Dude, we missed ya," close to my ear. His tightly bundled hairs tickle my cheek and neck. I let out a squeal as we release from our embrace and hold hands for a moment.

"Come and talk with us," I tell Phil as I attempt to slide toward the group's table. Our arms stretch out and hands finally release. He gathers his things and follows.

At the table, we get loud in our greetings and laughter as I take my pack off and find an empty seat.

"Molinaseca, eh?" says Deanna. "Where did you spend the god-awful storm?"

"Out in it, soaked and freezing," I say while feeling as stupid as my choice had been.

"My goodness, child," she says.

She waves over our waiter so I can order. I've had breakfast and have little money left. I touch the pocket where I keep loose change and a few bills. "Café con leche, por favor," I say to the squat young guy in his pressed white shirt. The coffee costs two euros. They are not my last. Not quite.

"Where are Beth and Howard?" I ask to the table.

Cheryl, seated far across the large table from Yan, answers. "They wanted to tour the Templar castle. We, *some of us*, didn't want to pay the admission price," she says while glaring at Yan. *Uh-oh.*

I can hear my coffee being made and the loud hiss of steam warming the milk. Two whole euros. Worth the cost, I assure myself.

The waiter brings the dainty cup to me on a little plate with packets of sugar, a little spoon, and the smallest possible biscuit. I'd call it an itty-bitty cookie.

"Macario tours the castle with them," says Phil with a wide, sugary grin.

He gets the response he expected. I squirm in my seat, turn pink, and act like I need something from my backpack. I dig around in there hoping to find a plausible item. When I look up, though, they all smile at me. "Okay, you guys. We are friends, will always be friends. He and I talked about it. Days and days ago. Only friends. You all know he is too old for me."

"And you are too young," says Deanna. Cheryl shakes her head, disagreeing about the age difference. Yan agrees with her. They tentatively smile at one another.

I take birdlike sips from the café con leche as they ask me about walking in the storm. Cheryl wants to know where I stayed last night. Deanna asks about Astorga, hoping I will tell more of my family's story. I occasionally get to ask my own questions, trying to understand how we all came together in this restaurant this morning. The whole thing is almost unexplainable. Cheryl and Yan took a taxi when the rain got too bad. Deanna has been here in Ponferrada for a couple of days waiting for Beth and Howard. She'd been "on a tear," as she put it and finally needed a break. Phil and Macario had stayed at Manjarín on the mountain, then made a mad dash to Molinaseca before the rain got too bad—they were inside the muni when I found the *COMPLETO* sign on its front door.

The questions fly in every direction and at rapid-fire pace. I'm about to lose it and run, when a group of pilgrims walks past on the sidewalk, pulling my attention to them. They are a blur, moving fast. One of them catches my eye. "Sara," blurts from my mouth.

She stops like she has hit a wall and turns in my direction. I get up and run out to her. We don't hug. If she were a hugger, she'd probably crush me. "Summer," she says with a tight tone in her voice. "How have you been, my surfer . . . girl . . . friend?" She has said these last three words as three separate sentences, like she's not too sure how I will receive them.

I smile reassuringly at her and look over her shoulder. "I'm good." I look back to her. "We're all here, at the same place and time. Those are my other friends," I say as I point out the people with curious faces looking at us. "We're all here. I can't believe it." But I can. I look past Sara again, to a line of muscled men behind her. Some with fresh flat-top haircuts, others unshaven and scruffy looking. At the far end, and up slope from us, waits an older man and a woman. She doesn't look like a soldier; their counselor, I assume.

Sara finally looks to where my friends are. They all wave. She looks down at me and smiles. It's not much of a smile.

I lean into her. "Are things okay, Sara?"

"Ah, sure. We've worked things out. Stages, you know. Talking at night over a campfire works magic." she replies while throwing a thumb in the direction of the veterans behind her. They stare. A couple of the guys have moved over so they can see me better. I hate the creepy grins on their faces. Sara becomes aware of this and turns to them. I can't see her face, but it said all that she wanted. The two men melt back into line and shy their faces away. *Not so badass, after all, eh boys.*

"I'd better get going," says Sara as she turns back to me. "They won't wait forever."

We shake hands and she pulls me to her body. It's not quite a hug. But for Sara this act of closeness is huge, I can tell.

"Buen Camino," I say. She returns the phrase and goes to her group. They march off in a line, weaving up the street like a snake on the hunt.

Before I get back to our table, I see the others perk up and look past me. Macario strides across the street. He circles his arms around but waits for me to pull him in before squeezing me tight. Over his shoulder are Beth and Howard, both with happy, the-gang's-all-here smiles on their faces. They wrap an arm across each other's shoulder and take it all in. I love these people.

Since leaving Ponferrada, Beth and I have been walking together, the rest of our group stretching out in front and behind us. The farms and beautiful homes dotting this valley look like I'd imagine heaven to look, if I believed in such things. Everything gleams and looks so alive, so healthy. I can barely remember how home in California looks. But I know it is dry there, almost dead in appearance this time of year. Even so, I love it there. Though it could use some rain real soon.

"Tell me more," says Beth. I come back to the present and to Spain.

I resume my storytelling. "Máire asked me to spend the night, said we could go to our grandfather's grave the next day. We talked late into the evening. She poured too much red wine. Next morning, she bought flowers, and we went to the cemetery where her parents and grandparents are."

Beth looks to me then over her shoulder. Cheryl and Yan are not far behind. They're not close or holding hands but are talking. Beth smiles at this.

"Why did she start sending the journal to California?"

"They're all gone. She's the last of her line. After her parents were killed, and she had moved into her grandparent's home, she read Georgia's journal. She read it and got curious. It took her some time to find Grandma Pat's address."

"Why the mystery? Why only a part of the diary at a time?"

"I didn't get a clear answer to that question. I think she thought doing so, sending it a piece at a time, her message would be taken seriously."

"She had no idea how seriously," says Beth. I nod in agreement.

The paved lane we walk on meanders through the gorgeous scenery. If they added a picture to the word *serenity* in a dictionary, I'm sure this is what you would see. Everything sparkles. A soft glow of amazing colors outlines all I can see. I feel myself wanting to slip back into camera view mode. Beth pulls me out of it.

"Will you go back to Astorga at some point?" she asks.

"Oh, yes. I'd love to. I want to bring Lou here. Bring her on Camino."

Beth smiles at the thought.

"How about your aunt? Will she ever come here?"

My head lowers, a sadness kills the glow on the things around us.

"Summer?"

I slowly look to Beth. I feel tears welling in the corners of my eyes.

"Oh, you poor thing."

I don't want people thinking of me as a poor thing.

Beth guides me a few yards off trail to a stone church. There are three horses and their riders in the grass beside the building. They had passed us earlier, me hardly noticing until Beth told me they ride their Caminos. They've stopped here to feed and water their animals.

She directs me to a bench near the front door to the church. "Let's sit for a while." We take off our backpacks and sit. "Can you tell me about her, your aunt?"

A twisted version of Tilly's mean face jumps into my mind. She still wants me to come home. Still holds tight, trying to control me. A column of numbers, all negative numbers replace her face in my mind's eye. They scroll by, slowly reminding me how little cash remains in the money belt buckled around my waist. "She wants me to come home, to get on a plane immediately, and come back to hold her hand."

"She must love you, no doubt worries about you," says Beth. The calmness in her voice doses the flames burning at the thought of Tilly getting her way.

"Tilly loves no one. Well, except for Louise," I say. "She hates when I call her daughter 'Lou'. Everyone uses her nickname. All of her friends."

Beth nods and sits quietly for a moment.

"Am I being selfish, do you think?" I ask.

"Selfish?"

"Yeah, am I doing the right thing by staying on the Camino?"

"Was it a good thing to come here? Was there good reason to?" she asks.

"I think so. Yes," I answer.

"Then, how can a good thing be taken as selfish?" she says

with a faraway look in her eyes. "Howard told you about his time in Iraq. I never fought in combat, but I've seen much of the outcome, the horrific effects of war. I'll say it again, how can something done for the sake of good, something drawing positive energy into our world get construed as a bad thing?"

I should write that one down. *Better start a journal, girl.*

Beth spins slightly around, now focused on my face. "When do you plan to walk into Santiago? How many days from now?"

"I have to arrive by the tenth, when my flight is," I answer. "But…"

Beth waits for me to continue. I can't. "But what?"

"I'm not sure I can make it that far."

"Why not? You're doing fine. We'll stay with you. You survived the storm and the first mountains," she says.

"I know. But. . . it's. . ." I'm still embarrassed. "I don't have much money left. Tilly turned off Grandma Pat's cards. I can't get more cash from an ATM." The tears start to flow. I'm not helpless. But I feel like it now.

"Oh," says Beth. "Hmm."

"She wants me to come back home so badly she'll. . ."

"Yes. I see," says Beth. I can see the wheels turning in her mind. Grandma Pat would smile.

"What can I do?"

"Well, let's look at it differently. You said your aunt doesn't understand what you do here. Doesn't care about her family here, that you have found her father. Am I correct?"

"Yes." Beth's a good listener.

"I find it helpful to come at difficult situations from a different angle," she says. "Do you know what I mean?"

"Yes, as an idea. But how? What new angle?" I ask.

"She hurts inside, you know. Has been hurting her whole life. Right?"

"Yeah, I suppose so," I say as I wonder where Beth is going with this.

"You hurt too."

I peer into her eyes, trying hard to understand.

"You miss your grandmother." I nod, more hot tears streaming from my face. "And I suspect you miss your parents, as well."

Her words hit like a hammer, turning on a light in my mind so bright it's blinding. I wipe the tears from my face and sit up straight. "Yes, of course I do."

Beth waits for it to all come together in my young mind. She'd have been a great mother.

By the time we come to the day's end at the town of Villafranca Del Bierzo, we have talked the subject into a complete plan.

"Tactics," I say aloud to Beth as we stroll into a huge, rectangular plaza.

"Strategy," replies Beth. We both smile. I feel hopeful for the first time in days.

Astorga, Spain
September 21, 1982

Father, after much discussion, agreed to show me his work. Sunday last, we went to his latest project, a remodel of a parochial school not far from the main square. As I had for market day, I promised to act like I didn't know him if we saw his friends on the street. I was to say I needed directions. Didn't go over well with me. But he explained the church and how Máire would get hurt if people knew about his other family. Well, I know how that feels.

From Georgia's Travel Journal

THIRTY-THREE

O Cebreiro, November 5, 2019

We climb high into the mountains again and enter our last *autonomous community*, what we would call a state. Galicia is famous for its rain and seafood and St. James. It's nearly dark and a cold breeze flips my hair about and into my eyes. Across a cobbled street from the municipal albergue, I'm sitting in the vacant patio of a café. At a table inside this place, my friends look warm. They laugh, happy and contented. Most of them. I can see Beth under the golden glow of a hanging lamp. She's worried about me, I can see it in her eyes.

I have a call to make. The Wi-Fi seems good here. The cold of the metal chair soaks into my behind.

I can't remember a more mysterious looking place. In the forest where I once lived, it felt dark and foreboding to some people. I knew those woods so well nothing ever frightened me. Well, except my father's friend, Paul. Here, though, it's like a film set for a medieval story, a dark tale. Moss hangs from huge, old trees, and drapes from stone walls and the roofs of the ancient buildings nearby. The scene has so much texture I could play this naming game all night. But I need to talk with Tilly.

I had texted Lou this afternoon that I would call this evening, my evening, their morning. I had imagined her squealing in delight. I followed up with a text saying I wanted to talk with her mother. Who knows how their conversation went? Not too good, I'm sure.

By now Tilly is ready to lash out at me again. To tell me what a horrible, selfish person I am.

I'm in a cold sweat when Lou clicks on. "Summer? You okay? It's so dark there."

"I'm fine, Lou. Is your mother there? Sorry. I have to do this right away or I'll hang up."

Tilly comes to the phone, her pudgy face filling the little screen in my hand.

"So, what do you want?" she asks. I can tell she really wanted to finish her question with her usual description of me. She has held her tongue. For once.

"I'm sorry about what your father did to you."

"That it?"

"You loved your sisters."

"That a question?" Ugh. She won't make this easy.

"I guess so," I say. There's a long pause. I wait, my hand beginning to tremble. I reach up with my other hand to steady the phone and wait.

"Well, I loved Pat, yes. Georgia, we never saw much of her, just like her father."

"Your father."

"Look, you litt—"

"Georgia found him." I cut her off quick as a mousetrap. "She lived with him for a while. Here in Spain. I saw where they lived, even stayed there one night."

There is a pause. "So what?" my great-aunt asks, though she's hesitant, her voice low.

"He had another family. In a place called Astorga."

Tilly gasps, draws in a ton of air, and looks about to explode. A thought screams into my mind while I wait for the cataclysmic event: Maybe the possibility of her father having a hidden life grew into her greatest fear. My aunt's face swells and turns red. The backlight in my phone worsens the effect. There is a glow about her, not the good kind. It's as red as her face, blurring at the edges of my screen.

"I can only think this news has hurt you, hurt you deeply. I'd think it devastating."

Tilly lets out a long sigh, deflating like a pot farmer who has found his crop dead from drought or sabotage.

"He, Grandfather Harold, found the peace here he could not find at home in the States. He married again." I pause for a moment, not sure how fast she can take in this news. Tilly's face looks drawn, her eyes moist. "They had a baby girl. She had a girl. I met her, the young one. She looks just like my mom." I stop.

"And what of it?" she says, not wanting to hear my response, but asking anyway.

"Are you still angry with him for leaving?"

"Of course, I am," she says, the tension in her voice rising then slipping away as she lets the words out.

I pull in a calming breath. "I'm angry at my Grandma Pat for leaving me, for dying. I'm also angry at my parents for not being real parents." Hot tears well up in my eyes. We probably look like the saddest pair of people on the planet right now.

Tilly lets out another long breath. "I don't want to hear any more of this, Summer. I have nothing more to say. I'm tired, exhausted. You need to come home," she says in a weak, powerless tone.

"I need to finish what we started. Grandma Pat would want me to do this. Santiago gets closer by the day. I will see you very soon." I am not about to ask her for money. I can't stoop so low. She knows what I need. I only hope she does the right thing.

She looks up. The red surrounding her face has disappeared. Though she can't see me very well, she's studying me. I think this is the first time she has ever truly looked at me, tried to understand me, my love for my grandmother. "How many days?"

"Five." There's a long pause as she continues to look at me through the little screen and the vast distance between us. I want to say more, but don't know what I could say. It's up to her now.

"Fine. Here's Louise," she says, and her face disappears from the screen.

Lou and I chat for a moment but say nothing, no life in our voices. She has heard it all; knows what I know, what her mother now knows. Before we say our goodbyes, Lou says, "I will talk with Mom."

It's almost too hot inside when I come to the table where my friends are. Macario pulls out a chair for me between him and Beth. He gives me one of his beautiful smiles then returns to his conversation with Phil and Celeste.

"How did it go?" asks Beth as she leans into my side.

I pick up the clean wine glass in front of me and hold it out.

"That bad, eh?" she says, frowning.

Howard reaches over with a carafe of red wine and half fills my glass. I top the red liquid with some water from a nearby pitcher. The waiter comes to take my order. I ask for the *ensalada mixta*, a mixed salad, usually an inexpensive meal in cafés like this. I let my talk with Aunt Tilly percolate in my mind. *How did it go?*

I turn to Beth and say, "As well as it could have, I guess."

She asks a couple more questions but doesn't pry when I am reluctant to talk about it.

My salad comes and I dig in. Macario hands me a basket of bread, a plate with butter on it, and a tall bottle of olive oil. Before long, I'm full. It feels great to feel full. I finish the wine in front of me and someone fills it again. I top this glass, as well, but don't think I'll drink any of the glistening liquid.

It's then I look around with better eyes. Cheryl and Yan are close again, their hands clasped together on the tabletop, fingers intertwined. Celeste and Phil, too, seem close. She's asking him to play his music. Macario sits by Deanna now, deep in a fun conversation, both smiling and happy. My favorite Spanish social butterfly and my favorite Canadian woman. Beth and Howard talk about tomorrow. I don't care about the future. I'll follow along for as long as I can. What more can I do?

Our waiter picks up plates and empty glasses. He's young, and handsome, in a shadowy way. His brown skin and the hint of a beard fit right in with this ancient place here in the mountains. I wonder if he was born here in mysterious and ancient O Cebreiro.

People's conversations ebb and flow around the table. Other pilgrim groups are leaving, going off to bed. I spin my wine glass with lithe fingers and let the murmur of voices and sounds of dishes being carted off soothe my mind. It's meditative, relaxing.

I am startled when my cell phone vibrates in my back pocket. Not really wanting to know what the message is, I slowly pull it out and set the phone on the table. Curiosity finally sinks in, and I unlock the smart-assed phone. There's a one-line text from Lou.

The credit cards should now work.

I almost fall over backward. Macario passes behind me and catches me. He was flittering to another seat somewhere around our table—to a different group, even. I thank him, and he moves on.

I text back to Lou.

What happened?

It's long moments before there's a response.

Mom put **TRAVEL ADVISORIES** back on each card.

I made sure she fixed them all.

Holy hell.

I hear muffled chatter to my right. Beth wraps an arm around me. "All good now?" I hesitate for a second and look into her eyes. "Howard said you were glowing again. This time in a good way."

"Yes. Everything is great now." I show her the series of texts and she squeezes me tight.

"Well done, young lady," she says with delight.

At least, she hasn't called me *little one.*

Astorga, Spain
September 24, 1982
As supper ended, Father asked me when I will return to the Camino de Santiago. I asked if he would ever finish the Way. "It's no longer a priority," he said. I saw the look he and his new wife shared at that moment. They are perhaps the happiest couple I have ever met. He's always so sad when she is not around, like there is only one light in his world. Father said I could stay; he was not asking me to leave soon. When will I go? Will I continue my Camino? Or find a new adventure? And what will I tell Mother and my sisters when I eventually get home? Father has asked me to say nothing.

From Georgia's Travel Journal

THIRTY-FOUR

Sarria, November 6, 2019

Our walk this morning is filled with good natured conversations. Mostly we talk about the Camino and our experiences, the people. We also discuss potential future adventures, other places in the world to visit and explore. Each place they mention, with familiar names or not, tickles at something inside of me.

The ability to talk and think about the future, my future, returned quickly after Tilly relented and left me to finish this trek for Grandma Pat.

I think of the many other Caminos in Europe that I have learned about. I would like to come with Lou next time, take a different route. I'm sure my cousin could use a break from her mother. We—Tilly and I—have talked again since I dropped the news on her about our Spanish family. In small bites, she listened to my stories from Astorga and the Camino. And I thanked her for returning my access to Grandma Pat's money.

In the village of Samos, I stop at an ATM. The others wait close by. Every muscle in my body tingles, tense in anticipation as I wait on the cash machine. As euro bills quickly stack up, relief floods over me like thick, warm chocolate syrup. My friends circle closer. Beth and Howard know the story, understand the reason for my anxiety and sudden relief. The others seem to have guessed that I had money troubles before this moment. I hold up the wad of cash in my hand and wave it about, a happy grin spread from ear to ear. They clap and cheer and pat me on a shoulder as we return to the Camino.

The group returns to our easy stroll, trekking poles ticking on the road as we leave town.

"We will come to Sarria before long," says Howard from several paces ahead.

Beth nods. "Big changes in the Camino from there."

Our group gathers in like a contracting spring. I'm the one to ask. "What kind of changes?"

"To earn a Compostela from the church when you arrive in Santiago, you must have walked or ridden a horse for at least one hundred kilometers of the Camino, any of them," says Howard.

"Or ridden a bicycle for a minimum of two hundred kilometers," adds Beth. "And you must have your pilgrim credential to prove your journey."

Howard agrees with a nod and continues. "Sarria is a major town and hub for pilgrims who don't have the time or money or health to walk a full Camino, and it's more than the required distance to Santiago. We will see many more pilgrims beginning this afternoon. More than we have seen anywhere before today."

Our gang of pilgrims comes to a highway and follows it, stretched out like a chain rattling with voices and the click-clack of trekking poles.

As we enter Sarria, and to prove his point, Howard suggests we have lunch at a pizzeria he remembers on the Rúa Maior, the main street where pilgrims will pass us by. We find a table on the patio and take our seats for the show. We've already seen many backpack-clad people who look "fresh off the train," as Howard says.

"Why would people come all this way for a hike of only a few days or a week?" I ask.

Cheryl takes this one. "Europeans, mostly Spaniards. It's easy to catch a train or two to get here from nearly anywhere in Europe."

"And they get their Compostela at the end of a weeklong vacation," I say as the concept gels in my mind.

Yan leans in. "Is truth," he says. "I take three trains from Sweden to Saint Jean, in Franca, before walking first Camino steps."

Howard has made sure I took a seat with the best angle to view the pilgrims walking past. He was right: A steady parade strolls by. Some have packs like ours. Most, though, have smaller daypacks or what some of them call *rucksacks*. After today, we have three more days of walking before we arrive in Santiago. This will get interesting, all these people on the trail and in the towns and in the albergues.

We have ordered and eventually our pizzas arrive. I hadn't noticed the time they took, conversations swelling and dying in waves around the table. The sight of grilled onions, melted cheese, Spanish ham, and a few olives immediately stops all conversation. Each one of us leans over and inhales the steam from the pies. We dive in, passing plates and swapping pizza slices.

Glancing over my pizza crust I can still watch pilgrims flow past. Many sing, joyful, fresh. Crowds stroll by in matching shirts, school or church groups, daypacks only.

Beth moves close and says, "It's okay. There are more people, but also more restaurants and albergues and hotels from here to Santiago. It all works out. You'll see."

"Oh, I'm not worried. Those days are behind me. I have cash now. I have great friends, both here and on the del Norte. And so much more," I say while feeling how true these words are.

"And there's *pulpo*," says Howard. Beth slaps his hand. He's grinning like a kid.

I'm about to ask what *pulpo* is when Beth says, "Never mind him. He gets silly in Galicia; he loves the seafood. Have you slept better recently? I know you eat better these days."

"Oh, yes. Everything seems great, now," I say.

"And you've had a chance to talk more with your aunt," she says.

"Yeah. She's still a pain in the you-know-what. But she listens. I've told her about my time on the north coast and the people I met on the Camino del Norte. I've been telling her about the churches and cathedrals Georgia loved so much. I explained the meseta. And I've described all of you to her and Lou."

"And how about your family in Astorga? Have you told her more about Máire?"

"Yeah. Some. She didn't want to hear it all, still doesn't. But when I told Lou about Máire and the cemetery and of the city, I could sense her mother there listening."

"You know what?"

"What."

"I'm happy for her, for your aunt, I mean."

I let her statement penetrate. It doesn't take long. "You're right. I bet she finally feels better about her father than . . . than ever in her whole life. Well, maybe not better, not good about him. But closure. Is that it?"

"Exactly."

"Grandma Pat would love this idea," I say. Beth smiles and a warm, golden glow dances around her.

As I munch on pizza and sip from a cola, my mind spends time back in the States. Where will I be allowed to live? Will Tilly leave me on my own but act as my guardian? What will my parents have to say about my future? A warmth from within consumes me. I set down the scrap of crust in my hands. For the first time in years—if ever—I miss my parents.

Before it gets too late, we finish off the last slices of pizza and step into the flow of pilgrims going west. Howard says we have thirteen miles until we get to Portomarín, tonight's planned sleepover.

Our path continues. I barely notice it passing underfoot.

During the last couple of days, Galicia has been gorgeous and verdant, Deanna's word. But I, sadly, have not focused on much of its beauty. I know I should, I don't want to miss any of the Camino. But life has been a blur of talking with my friends, eating, looking for clean drinking water, and ducking from an occasional cloudburst.

Howard and the others had pulpo last night in the town of Melide. I tried a few of the rubbery bites of octopus. I thought it okay. I could try it again before returning to the States. Howard devoured his plate and half of Beth's. "Pulpo is famous here. It's like their regional specialty," he'd said around a bite of the tentacled creature before washing it down with a gulp of white wine.

Much has changed in the world around me, and for me. More pilgrims, of course. Also, a renewed vigor in our steps, yet a pull to savor every moment. And today I've been texting back and forth on WhatsApp with Rond and Cheng and Sofia.

Beth comes up to me, Macario is on the opposite side. They grin at me. "What?" I ask.

"You seem distracted, off in another world again, that's all," says Beth. I look from her to Macario. How has she enlisted him into her maternal role? He smiles wide, beautiful as always.

"I've been busy," I say to them. They wait for more. "I'm texting my Camino del Norte family."

"Dónde— Where are they?" asks the handsome, not-young-enough Spaniard.

"They are close. You may meet them later today," I say. "The Norte comes into the Francés at the town of Arzúa, not far ahead of us."

"Then we join forces," quips Beth.

"And together we carry our beautiful Lady Summer to victory," says Macario with a flourish of waving hands, like he's a court jester, which he often is.

Beth laughs, Macario laughs, then our whole group has stopped in the path, blocking the flow of pilgrim traffic.

Before getting out of people's way and moving on, I tell the rest of our group about our catching up with some of my other friends. Afterward, I pay more attention to the scenery, cows being herded along winding village streets, our path, where it leads us through deep troughs worn into the earth by the millions of pilgrim feet treading the Way before us.

Six miles past Arzúa, we catch up with the Norwegian and his group of pretty women. Cheng is the first to look back and see me. She calls out. She's squealing loudly as we jog into each other's arms. Sofia and Eugenia join in our happy dance. There are a couple of new faces in their group. Beyond them, Rond stands. He looks so different, sort of confident. I hardly believe he's the same guy I met a few weeks ago, in a different place, in another world almost.

The girls let go of me and open their circle to Rond. He comes close. I smile, and say, "Hola, mi amigo."

"Hola, blue eyes." We hug tight and both start talking at the same time. I want to tell them everything that has happened. I want to hear their stories too. My Camino Francés family surrounds me. We're like this huge atom of particles spinning in the road—blocking the path again for anyone else still wishing to walk toward Santiago.

Astorga, Spain

September 25, 1982

I called home yesterday. Also kept my promise to Father. Today, I have decided the Camino de Santiago no longer calls me. After talking with Mother, I miss home for the first time. Patricia has gone away to college, only seen again during the holidays. Mother says she needs help with Tilly, my sullen, troubled sister. Perhaps I'll come back here one day. Who knows? There are so many places to see in the world.

From Georgia's Travel Journal

THIRTY-FIVE

Santiago, November 9, 2019

A large SANTIAGO de COMPOSTELA sign on a wall of dark green ivy comes into view as we carefully skirt around a busy traffic circle at the outskirts of Santiago. Beth and Howard, and Sofia and Eugenia have decided they will walk together to the sea at Finisterre after a couple of days rest in Santiago. Rond has to go home, get back to his studies. I probably need to appease my aunt and go home. She has let me be, has let me finish what her sisters and their father had set out to do. I only have a mile or two more to the plaza and the Cathedral of Santiago.

"It's a frisson, isn't it?" says Deanna as she strolls beside me.

"A what?" I ask.

"This feeling, this excitement we all feel. It's palpable," she says, then laughs at her own silliness.

I get it. We all feel the buzz. "But there is a melancholy, too,"

I toss back at her and smile. We laugh together at our joke. The others join us in our laughter, not even knowing why.

They, my Camino families, have me surrounded again. And I love it, love them. Which adds to the layer of true melancholy in my emotions right now. Tomorrow, I will take a flight from the Santiago airport. I will miss these people—old and young, tall and short, social butterflies and timid mice, counselors and spirit guides—every single one of them.

This sad feeling spreads. We walk along quietly, all of us, for the first time in days. No one says a word. Horns toot in the distance. Trucks rumble up and down a busy road. A mist floats down from the gray skies. The damp surroundings smell like a city, but somehow odd: Exhaust fumes and wet roads and damp flowers. Human smells too. We didn't have these odors on the meseta or at the beaches, not in the cathedrals or churches, though they were often musty. Santiago proves its differences to us as we finish this journey.

Macario can no longer stand it. He runs ahead, turns back to us, and shouts, "We celebrate tonight, yes?"

We all cheer and start talking again. It's time to party.

As we enter the older parts of the city the streets narrow and the architecture of old Spain comes into view, warming my heart. Howard points them out—we can now see the spires of the cathedral reaching high above the rooftops.

The sound of bagpipes reminds me of my new-found relative in Astorga. Máire told me about this entrance to the plaza at the end of the Camino. She has not been here herself, but wishes to see this sight one day. She and Lou and I could walk together through this tunnel. Someday soon, I hope.

We—I look around, now fifteen or more of us—step out of the muted light in the tunnel and onto the plaza, Praza do Obradoiro. We walk among and around other groups of pilgrims and tourists to the center of the huge square. People hug, cheer, take pictures; some hold up national, regional, and ethnic flags. Some are tearful, though there isn't a sad face anywhere in the crowd.

We gather and whoop and yell. Macario grabs me and kisses me on the forehead. Close by, Celeste swings in Phil's long arms. Deanna records the happy event with her smartphone. Cheryl and Yan hug. Beth and Howard hug. We turn and face the cathedral, squeezing together in a tight cluster, pulling together in a tangled mess of a group hug.

I'm deep in the center, too many voices at once. I can't understand much of what is said, and don't try too hard. A hush falls over the crowd, and our dance calms. I can hear other groups shouting and calling out greetings as more pilgrims arrive in the plaza.

My friends ease away. I take it all in and stop. At the outer edge, Howard and Macario have moved apart, the others follow. A path opens before me. There stands a tall man outside of our jagged circle. I can't quite see his face in the low light. He's in gray robes, an old brown belt around his middle.

"Father Ernesto?" I say, yet do not believe what I think I see. He smiles and waves a hand toward another man in robes beside him. "Father Emil?"

My friends look at me and smile. I glance to each face, unable to explain the scene.

The two priests step closer to me, admitted with false officiousness by our gatekeepers.

My eyes blur with hot tears which immediately stream down my face. My view is from inside again, through the camera's lens. The other people who have helped me to get here appear on the surface of this blurred mess of liquid covering the lens. The scene is like a film played out on a fuzzy, waving sheet hung from the sky. I can see Maria, the wonderful blister healer; there's Memo, his scruffy gray hairs, and his sagging sofa; the helpful monk at an old monastery out in the countryside hundreds of miles from here; and dear cousin Máire and her amazing friend Priscilla.

Father Ernesto now has my hands in his.

"How in the . . .?" I begin.

"We have kept track of your progress, my child," says Father Emil from over Ernesto's shoulder.

"We had help," says Father Ernesto with a light tone.

"The Camino provides," I say.

"In many ways," says Father Ernesto.

I begin the task of introductions. Beth stands back but has a happy, lustrous glow around her. She smiles and winks at me when she sees me eyeing her.

Howard comes to us, a young man in tow. "This is . . . What is your name, young man?"

"Benjamin, sir," says the boy.

"Benjamin, here, will take a group photo for us," says Howard, and pauses. As soon as I smile and nod my understanding, Howard starts directing. He's shouting over everyone, waving his arms around, organizing us into neat rows. Beth follows orders and rejoins us.

"Summer," Howard calls. "Sit here, in the middle."

Our backpacks sit stacked in a heap, and I rest on them where I'm told. The rows slowly come into shape. I look around.

"Father Ernesto!" I shout.

"Right behind you," says Howard from in front of our gang.

I look in the direction Howard's pointing in. The old priest appears uptight, guarded. He looks down, and I smile warmly when our eyes meet. His shoulders drop lower as the tension in his body eases. He smiles back. Father Emil stands beside him. Beth is placed beside me on one side, Macario on the other. Howard is finally pleased with his work. He turns and says something to his volunteer photographer, then turns back to us.

"Okay, ready everyone?" Satisfied, he goes to one end of our group.

Benjamin looks tentative but slides one way and another, lifting one of the phones now in his possession. He could run off with about ten smartphones right now. The group closes in, and Howard says, "Now, everyone."

They all swing their arms and hands toward the middle, pointing at me. I try to smile, but blush instead. My head swivels and searches for the smiling faces of each of my friends. They are so happy. I am so happy right now. I only wish those cameras could capture the brilliant glow that surrounds us.

Before long, the mist from the skies turns to rain and the plaza begins to clear.

As we head for cover, I tell the two priests in our disorderly group about the albergue where we plan to stay tonight. "Where do you stay?" I ask as I look to them both.

Father Ernesto takes my elbow and leans down as we walk back into the tunnel. "I have arranged a tour of the cathedral for you this evening. And your friends, if they would like. Later, you will go and have a good evening. You will have much fun as you celebrate the completion of the Camino. First, though, you should collect your Compostela."

"Yes," says Beth as she comes up beside me. "We should go to the Pilgrim's Office soon. The line stretches long sometimes."

"I wasn't planning to get mine," I say.

Father Ernesto scowls at me for the first time. "You must. You have earned it, have done so much. You will want it when you are home—to remind you."

I lower my gaze. "Remind me? How can I forget my time here?"

"Come on, we're going to the office together, to get our Compostelas," says Howard. "We'll keep this party going, right, everyone?" A cheer goes up. "The office first, then the cathedral with Father Ernesto." Another hail and waving arms from the group.

I'm excited about the cathedral tour. Neither Great-grandfather Harold nor Aunt Georgia made it this far. And I'm sad that Father Ernesto will not be with us tonight but understand he cannot join the party the others have in mind.

As this thought spins in my mind, I look ahead and can see Macario and Beth and Phil, their heads together, planning, as I imagined they would.

We set a time to meet Fathers Ernesto and Emil at the cathedral and begin to follow Howard toward the Pilgrim's office.

The line is long, but we each take a number and find a place out of the rain to wait our turn. Howard hands me his number and takes mine. "You're up first."

Several minutes later, the number in my hand comes up on the board.

The tall, elderly man with a French accent behind the counter asks me a few questions, lifts out the colorful form from a stack at his side, and reviews the stamps, or *sellos*, on my pilgrim credential. He is confused and asks more questions. It takes him a moment to understand my two Caminos. He gets up and goes to ask for advice from a supervisor. When the tall man has an answer, he returns. On the form, he writes *Norte/Francés*. He looks it over, satisfied. He asks, since I have walked so many miles, if I want the distance certificate too. I hesitate but think of Beth and Howard. I nod my head, and he begins filling out an additional form.

With the completed Compostela and distance certificate in hand, I thank the man and return to our group in the hall. They are happy to see my smile. The pages of thick paper are beautiful, written in Latin calligraphy, Beth tells me, and have colorful, flowery borders on one side and top. I guess I thought the Compostela would be a boring, plain piece of paper. But these will get a special place in my room—wherever I end up living. A few more in our group still wait for their turn to come.

I slip away, take off my pack, and slide down a wall to sit. As I try to understand the documents, thoughts about my future filter into my mind again.

How are my father's crops this year? How is my mother taking the news about her mother? And what about Paul? Has someone finally put him in his place? My view of the documents in my hands goes blurry. An aura of blue surrounds my hands. What *will* happen when I go home?

More damn questions.

Celeste is the last to receive her Compostela and distance certificate. Someone suggests tapas and vino before we meet the two priests for our tour of the cathedral. My stomach growls.

An hour later, we find Father Ernesto and Father Emil at the main entrance near Praza das Praterías. Ernesto leads us past a group of children and their chaperones standing near the doorway and into the old building. Scaffolding and temporary walls of draped plastic taint the occasion. Noises from restoration work taking place out of sight remind me of San Sebastián—and my grandmother. She wasn't happy with all that noise. "Racket" she had called it. And I'm not pleased by the racket here, today.

Father Ernesto quickly leads us across the cathedral to find a quiet corner. We are met by another priest. He will give the tour. Introductions go around and we start following him and Father Ernesto. I look back and see Father Emil herding our slackers. The tour is in Spanish. Father Ernesto translates. We are taking what they call the "Night Visit" tour.

Aunt Georgia and Grandma Pat, a golden hue surrounding their ethereal bodies, stroll along at my side, listening intently to the priests. My heart glows. A soft red luminance emanates from my chest. *Camino de Santiago, what have you done to me?*

Astorga, Spain
September 27, 1982

Closing words to my journal: I promised Father I would keep his secret. I've come to understand him, maybe even love him again. I can never know his pain, though I can see it in his dark, sad eyes. I also see the love he has for his Spanish wife. So, to you, my journal, I close your pages, my record of 1982, never to look upon them again. I shall leave you here in my father's home. And I hope it's found one day far from now. On a day when it no longer matters it will find its way to Patricia, my best sister, my best friend.

From Georgia's Travel Journal

THIRTY-SIX

Santiago, November 10, 2019

The bus ride from the city center to the airport is a blur. My mind has returned to the cathedral and our time with Father Ernesto last evening. I had so many questions for my friend, the priest. As we strolled through our tour, I asked how he managed to be in Santiago at the right time to meet us in the plaza. I asked if he had anything to do with the help I received at a lonely monastery before the meseta. In response, he merely shrugged his shoulders. The spirits of Aunt Georgia and Grandma Pat grinned as the priest toyed with me.

He asked his own questions: Did I find the Camino different from what I had expected? Did my aunt make it back to California okay? Did I ever feel or experience Camino magic?

I told him about my time at Eunate. He knew the old, oddly shaped church. I gave him a shortened version of what Tilly had done to Grandma Pat's credit cards, of Beth's advice, and the outcome. And I gave him a rundown on Georgia's journal, how it had led me to her father, my great-grandfather. With each story, he nodded as an elder would when receiving a report from a subordinate.

In the end, Father Ernesto said he had to catch a train in the morning, which would "whisk" him back to "San Sebastián and the Buen Pastor Cathedral."

I love the way he talked, the words he used. Love how he had helped me and my family after Grandma Pat had died. Love him for the assistance he wouldn't admit to organizing. And I love him for taking the time to join us there in the plaza yesterday. Also, for being in our group photos—however reluctant he may have been.

As I stand in line waiting for my turn, thoughts of Georgia rise again. She saw the world, but she also took time to find her father, to learn to love him again. I don't know what the future looks like, no one does. But I know what I will do.

Now it's time to leave Spain. I'm next in line at the airline service counter. I'm being called by an agent down the line.

"Good morning. Where do you go?" she asks with richly accented English.

I hand over a printout Grandma Pat had given to me with my flight details and say, "Can I change my flight to the US?"

"What is your new final destination?" she asks as she starts typing on a keyboard.

"Seattle Washington, not San Diego."

"What is in Seattle?" she asks, making conversation.

"I'm going to visit my parents."

Acknowledgments

No one gets to the top of a mountain by themselves. So many wonderful people have been part of the success of *Camino Child* that I don't know where to start. How about in the beginning? A huge thanks and a bear hug to Mike Addis for suggesting the premise for this story. Mike and I and another buddy were hiking the Pacific Crest Trail in 2018. Mike had listened to my tales from the Camino de Santiago and of my newfound passion for writing. One day he blurted out "Why don't you write about a young girl who finds herself walking the Camino alone." I've been immersed in this story since the very moment.

Early in the process, the Scripsit critique group, of which I am a member, helped bring focus to the story's opening and eventual outline. Many thanks to John, Marta, Marion, Margaret, Mark, and Terry.

Of great value is having a writing coach (who also inspired part of the storyline in *Camino Child*) and completed the final copyediting. Thank you, Amber Lea Starfire, author of *Journaling for Dummies* and many other books, for everything you do.

A huge shout out to Camino friend Steve Watkins, author of *Pilgrim Strong*, for his encouragement and advice on so many levels. Steve and I met through social media but have become good friends since then. Through Steve, I met other inspiring folks, who ultimately became part of this project, including James L. (Jim) Rubart, Rubart Writing Academy and Cristy Hall of Fame author, and Beth Jusino, author of *Walking to the End of the World* and developmental editor.

Through the worldwide Camino community, I have met hundreds of amazing people and pilgrims. One is Kevin Craig, author of *The Camino Club*. Kevin offered to give my novel a read through. He is an amazing writer and all-around good guy. I hope we meet in person someday; I'd love to shake his hand.

Others in the Camino community who added to the final product or have been part of my platform building and marketing include, well-known pilgrim Johnniewalker Santiago, Dan Mullins, at *My Camino the Podcast*, and Leigh Brennan, at *The Camino Café* podcast.

I love my beta readers and all their help pointing out issues and suggesting word/language changes. Hugs to Layla Wall (my favorite young traveler), Sarita Lopez (then president of Napa Valley Writers), LaDonn Morgan-Garcia (a close friend and one of my favorite cheerleaders), Janice Hinterman (an educator who hears what language young people use more than I do) and Meg Maloney (author of *Slow Your Roll*).

Last but not least, hugs to Mom Crothers for her everlasting encouragement, and a big smooch to my wife, Kathey, for putting up with all my time away researching Camino locations and those many hours of writing, rewriting, editing and sometimes being depressed over a plot hole or two (maybe more).

About the Author

Brien Crothers has traveled to dozens of countries, on five continents; climbed highest mountains, backpacked South America, raced across Vietnam, parts of the Sahara (Morocco) and Ina (Peru) deserts on foot, mountain bike raced in South Africa, and walked more that 1,700 miles in Europe and visited more cathedrals than you can imagine. Along the Way, Brien found a passion for writing and creating stories to encourage others to travel and expand their boundaries.

Find more at briencrothers.com

https://www.facebook.com/brien.crothers.author

https://www.instagram.com/briencrothersauthor/

https://twitter.com/BrienCrothers

Made in the USA
Columbia, SC
13 March 2023